P9-DFX-024

COMMONWEALTH OF KENTUCKY
UNITED WE STAND
DIVIDED WE FALL

The Legend of
ROLAND

I Charlemagne between Roland and Oliver. The Emperor's halo is a sign of his sainthood; he was canonized in 1165.

The Legend of ROLAND
a Pageant of the Middle Ages

D. D. R. OWEN

PHAIDON

Phaidon Press Limited, 5 Cromwell Place, London SW7

Published in the United States of America by Phaidon Publishers Inc.
and distributed by Praeger Publishers Inc.
111 Fourth Avenue, New York, N.Y. 10003

First Published in 1973

ISBN 0 7148 1546 2

Library of Congress Catalog Card Number: 73-179923

Printed in Belgium by Loiseau S.A. Brussels

Contents

Preface

WITH ROLAND France found her great national hero. We know that twelve hundred years ago he served Charles, King of the Franks, only to meet his death in a military disaster high in the Pyrenees. Some three centuries later his deeds were celebrated in a superb epic song in the Old French tongue that has come down to us in a single modest manuscript copied and preserved in England. This can hardly have been the starting point of his legend; it was far from being its final form.

In my first chapter I shall attempt to set not only Roland but Charlemagne too and the legend that so intimately connects them within their historical context. The second and main section of the book will give an account of the *Song of Roland* in words and pictures. The illustrations, assembled from many medieval sources, are arranged as far as possible so as to provide a visual accompaniment to the events told in the epic, with lines from my translation (quoted by courtesy of Messrs. George Allen and Unwin) serving as captions. A third chapter will present more briefly some of the legendary exploits that attached themselves later to Roland's name. For throughout the Middle Ages this was a name that reverberated in men's imaginations like the sound of his own mighty horn-call in the Spanish hills. Even today its echoes stir the soul.

II The warriors of Charlemagne's army setting out for Spain wear long suits of mail over tunics and helmets with nasals. The same soldiers are shown below, much aged after the long campaign. They have laid aside their battle array and are walking again in the street of Aix where Charlemagne, according to the *Pseudo-Turpin Chronicle*, made new buildings on his return from Spain. The dome of his cathedral is shown in the bottom left, with, below it, a corner of chequered Carolingian marble pavement. This has, in fact, since been excavated in Aix.

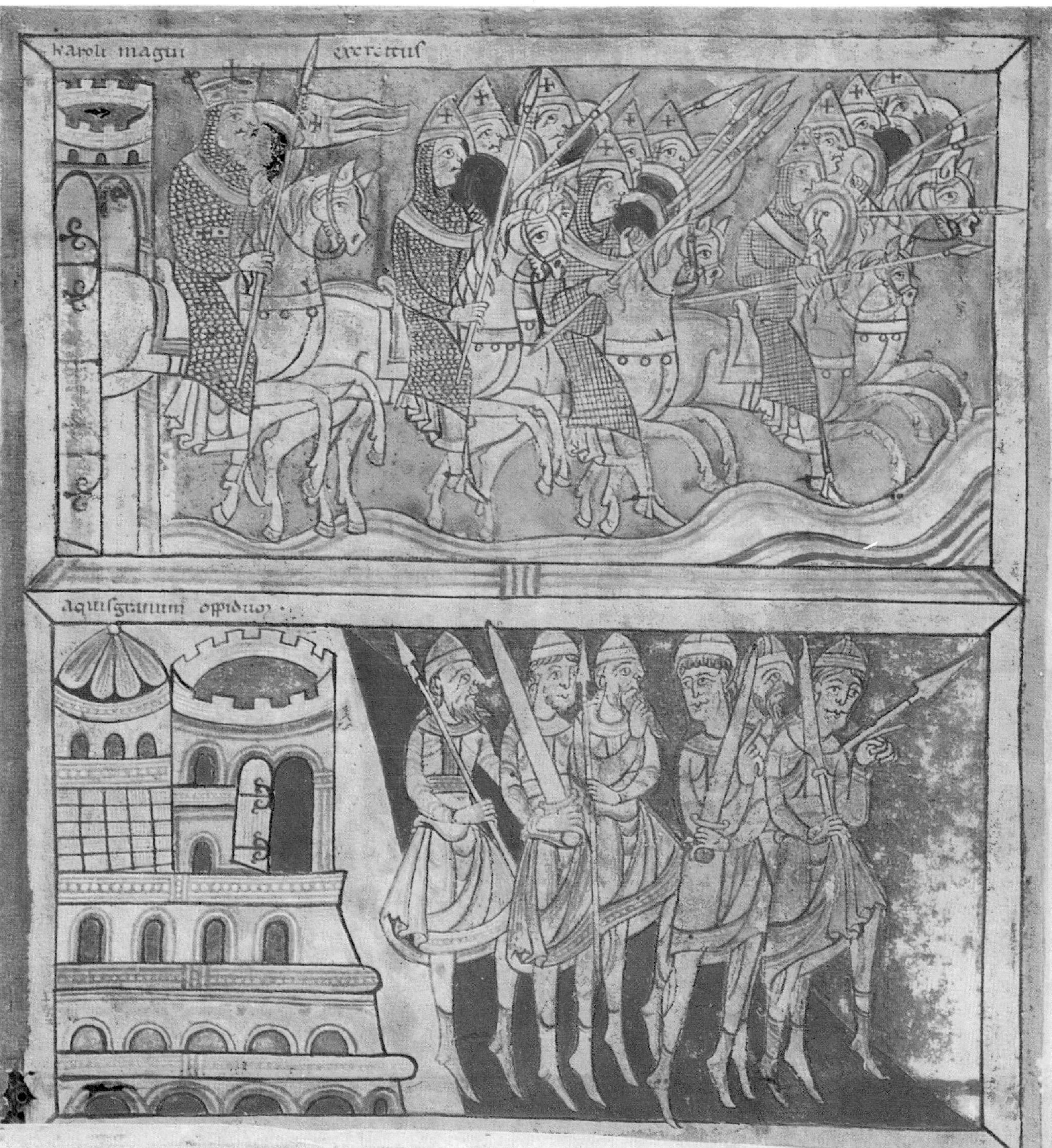
Karoli magni exercitus
aquisgranum oppidum

Facts and Fictions

FRANKS AND SARACENS

ACROSS THE ROMAN EMPIRE in the fifth century swept the tide of Germanic invasions. Within a hundred years the greater part of colonial Gaul fell under the domination of the Franks, and it was from them that France was to take its name. They did not displace the existing population, but they were the masters and theirs was the law. Only in the matter of language did they eventually submit, yet not without leaving an indelible mark on the Latin tongue, the true mother of French; and among the hundreds of words they have bequeathed to the Frenchmen of today are terms that seem to speak of the fierce Frankish character, words like those for 'war' and 'arrogance', 'hate' and 'shame'.

They were a proud and combative people with tight, clannish loyalties, which were not lessened by their minority position in their new home. Family honour was for them a matter of the gravest importance, and it appears that the uncle–nephew relationship held a special significance. Roman justice, though they came to terms with it, did not dull their inherited instinct for the blood feud or the examination of a case through trial by combat. When they espoused Christianity, it was in a form remote from the gentle creed of the early Fathers, being inflamed with their own barbaric morality. Treachery and bad faith were in their eyes the ultimate, though not unpractised, sin; courage, loyalty, skill in arms and on horseback were the highest virtues. These were the people destined to form the feudal aristocracy of France, with their power rooted in the lands they gathered to themselves and held more or less under the suzerainty of their kings. They were the ancestors of the Christian warriors we shall see riding through the pages of this book: the forebears of Roland, of Charlemagne—and of the traitor Ganelon.

Clovis, who died in 511, united Gaul under the Franks. But the Merovingian line he established was fated to tear itself apart with internecine scheming and feuding. Culture declined with

1 The battle of Roncevaux. In this stylized representation of the conflict between good and evil, the Christians stand on the left, a solid phalanx, resolutely directing their lances at the heathen who stride towards them brandishing their spears, eyes flashing in dark faces beneath their turbans, with fierce grimacing heads on their shields.

2 Turpin baptizing the Spanish infidels. Forcible conversion was a feature of the religious crusades against the Moors. Here Charlemagne's archbishop with an acolyte is performing the rites over a neophyte immersed to his neck in a large font. On the right stand Christian sponsors.

the royal authority; and the land, disputed by its princes, ran with blood. Typical is the fate of the power-hungry Queen Brunhilde, who ended her days like Ganelon, dragged at a wild horse's tail. Ultimately, the Frankish dominion was preserved only by the intervention of a family of court officers, the mayors of the palace; and one of them, Pepin the Short, eventually took to himself the kingship of all the Franks in the year 751. The Carolingian dynasty had replaced the Merovingian. For Pepin's son Charles history and legend were to reserve one of their most glorious chapters. We know him as Charlemagne.

Of all the pressures and threats to which the Merovingians had been subjected, whether from inside or from outside their territory, there is one that has particular interest for us—the menace of Islam. Mohammed died in 632: a hundred years later his followers were at the very throat of the Frankish kingdom, having conquered vast lands to the east and south of the Mediterranean and gained a firm foothold in western Europe by wrenching Spain from the Visigoths. The Moslems followed up this success by probing beyond the Pyrenees. Carcassonne, Nîmes, the whole of Gascony suffered from their ravages. Then in 732 they reached Poitiers, burnt the church of St. Hilary, and threatened to advance on Tours. But in Charles Martel, Pepin's father and himself virtual ruler of the Franks, they met their match. Outside Poitiers he defeated them in battle and so put a firm end to their northward penetration. It was left to Pepin to clear them from the south of France, at least for the time being; and in 759 Narbonne, the last of the Saracen strongholds there, was taken. But the Moslems were still in Spain and remained a potential danger to their Frankish neighbours.

Plate 1

On Pepin's death in 768 the kingdom was divided between his two sons, the twenty-six-year-old Charles and the younger Carloman. Three years later Carloman died, and Charles took the crown of the whole *regnum Francorum*. He was to rule as king and emperor until his death in 814, rich in years and the knowledge that through his statesmanship and tireless energy he had erected a political edifice for the world to admire. For by then he was not merely monarch of the Franks, but had built for them an empire stretching from northern Spain to Hungary and the heart of Europe, and in the south to Calabria. On Christmas Day in the year 800 the seal had been set on his career when in Rome Pope Leo III had crowned him as the first of the line of Holy Roman Emperors. Charles was now truly Charlemagne, Charles the Great.

Plates I, *99*

His physical and mental vigour were enormous. No stay-at-home monarch, this: his whole court moved from place to place at the call of events, and even his chief seat at Aix-la-Chapelle was anything but a permanent residence. Where his armies went on their great campaigns, Charles went too; and though he seldom fought with them in the field, he was there to control strategy and inspire the men with his presence, riding tirelessly through his lands, as much at home on horseback as on a throne.

Frankish infantry did exist, but most of his troops were mounted. Their armour consisted of helmet and byrnie, a padded leather jacket sewn with metal plates or links. Long lances were carried, which they would normally hurl at the enemy before drawing their great double-edged swords and fending off return blows with their round shields. Small standards or gonfalons were often carried into battle at the lances' tips.

When the king himself was not at the head of his warriors, they would be led by one or other of his chief nobles, many of whom had been trained in the royal household, and who could be trusted to carry through an expedition with loyalty and despatch. They ranged throughout Europe, defending the homelands of the Franks or forcing submission and, if need be, the Christian faith on peoples outside their borders.

Charles's first task had been to quell a revolt in Aquitaine; but before long he is found operating against the Lombards in Italy and, with papal approval, asserting Frankish authority over much of that country. It was the pagan Saxons, however, who proved the sharpest thorn in his flesh, a folk no less hard and fierce than his own. For much of his reign he was either warring against them, compelling them to abandon their old gods and submit to his rule, or else looking anxiously towards their eastern territories for signs of further trouble.

Plates 2, 25

It was because of the Saxon threat that he was unable for many years to take retribution for his humiliation in Spain, the chief subject of our legend. He had invaded that land in 778, thinking to render Aquitaine once and for all secure from Saracen attack; but as things turned out, it was almost twenty years before the Spanish march, modern Catalonia, was established, eventually to be attached to Aquitaine. In the interval, the Moors had forced their way once again into France, raided Narbonne and marched on Carcassonne, inflicting a defeat on Count William of Toulouse that was to form one of the most poignant episodes in later epic song. As for the Saxons, their final subjugation was not achieved until near the end of the century.

Plate II

This was by no means the sum of Charles's campaigns. There were difficulties with the Bavarians that had to be resolved. Further east the Slavs and Avars were uneasy neighbours; indeed we are told that only the Saxon wars were more bitter than the eight-year struggle to reduce and Christianize the Avars. In northern Italy, clashes with the Byzantine Greeks plagued the final years of Charles's reign, while at the other extremities of his empire we find the Bretons giving trouble, and naval warfare being engaged with the Saracens in Mediterranean waters. Small wonder that legends of Charlemagne the hero-king were to live long.

Only a man of his colossal stature could hope to hold the Frankish empire together. In the event, within thirty years of his death it was dismembered by his successors, and jealous rivalries ate into the heart of the Carolingian state, while its body suffered grievously at the hands of a series of invaders.

Once again the Saracen sword was turned against the Franks. Their piratical bands came marauding along the Mediterranean coast: in Italy St. Peter's itself was sacked, and in France for well over a century the southern littoral and the Rhone valley were exposed to raids and even small-scale occupation. Towns like Arles were plundered, captives and slaves taken, ransoms exacted. The Franks had good cause to look upon the men of Islam as their natural foes. *Plate 3*

Meanwhile, in the north the Viking wave was already breaking with equal ferocity and more permanent effect, for it was the Norsemen who seized and gave their name to the province of Normandy. Nor were the eastern borders any more secure, as the ravages of Hungarian war-bands showed. These were truly dark times; and the Carolingian dynasty itself tottered to its fall, to be replaced by the Capetian line in 987. When in that year Hugh Capet became king of the West Franks, hindsight tells us that the history of France as a nation had begun. National sentiment and patriotism, however, despite the appearance in the *Song of Roland* of a spirit that looks very like it, was far from existing in its familiar, modern form. For with the Capetians we are firmly in the age of feudalism.

There is no finer illustration of the feudal ethos than that found in the Roland legend. The system, born in these dangerous times of the necessity for freemen to seek the protection of more powerful neighbours, had evolved over many years. The greater nobles too needed men on whose service they could depend, and for this they were prepared to pay in land, the basic wealth of the age. So the granting of fiefs was at the very base of feudalism, with the king bestowing them on his chief vassals, they on lesser nobles, and so on down to tenant farmers for whom the serfs laboured.

The arrangement brought mutual advantages to lord and vassal, but it involved mutual obligations too. Fulbert, Bishop of Chartres, wrote in 1020 of the vassal's duties towards his lord: he must do no injury either to his person or to anything pertaining to his security, honour, or property; and more positively, he is obliged to be always ready to advise and aid him. But Fulbert emphasizes that the lord in turn has to observe these same obligations towards his vassal; otherwise he would be guilty of bad faith. This was the crux of the matter: honour and loyalty had to be reciprocal if the arrangement was to work and the system to survive. To encourage this, the swearing of homage and investiture of the fief was endowed with a solemn ritual backed by the sanction of religion. God was the supreme overlord, the king his vice-regent; and it was in the divine scheme of things that there should be three social orders: the fighting knights, the praying clerics, and the toiling commoners.

God was also the final dispenser of justice. When human law or the royal court failed to produce a clear verdict in disputes between vassals, the divine judgment might be sought through judicial combat. Ermoldus Nigellus, describing the practice in about 827, has left a picture that corresponds remarkably with the great *Roland*-poet's account, almost three centuries later, of the Ganelon affair:

> There was and still is an ancient custom of the Franks which, so long as it lasts, will be the honour and glory of that people: when any man fails to keep faith with the king, for reward or by deceit, or when the wretch seeks to perform against the king, his family or his authority an act in contravention of his pledged faith, and if then a fellow subject presents himself declaring that he too is concerned with this matter, it is right that they should both fight it out in a fierce duel in the presence of the Frankish kings and all the court; for France abhors this crime.

A particular case is mentioned:

> The emperor declares: 'The Franks may settle this affair: it is right and fitting and is also our command'. And when the Franks' judgement has been passed according to the ancient custom, they [the contestants] prepare their arms and quiver with impatience to get to grips.

If effective justice was the vital buttress of the whole feudal edifice, loyalty and good faith were its cement. Consider the duties of a typical noble. He was bound by the ideals of family honour as well as blood to his own kith and kin. He was responsible for the welfare of all who served under him, from the serfs who tilled his fields to the troops he commanded in battle. To his overlord, the king himself in the case of the great barons, he owed support at all times, whether in the form of counsel or by the provision of men and material in the hour of need. For his conduct in all these matters he was answerable not only to his fellows but to God, stern judge of the renegade and traitor, and no friend of the man who, insensitive to the vital feudal constraints and obligations, fell prey to the sin of *démesure*, that excessive self-assertion that breeds intemperate acts.

There was yet another bond, and a very personal one, that knights might freely assume and observe. This was the tradition, deep-rooted it seems in Frankish custom, of comradeship or brother-

3 The heathens made forays to reconquer Spain from Charlemagne. Here in an episode from the *Pseudo-Turpin Chronicle,* a raiding party led by King Agolant meets with resistance from Christians in a beleaguered city. The small figure in the tower, with the lion on his shield, is Roland.

4 Archbishop Turpin and, on the right, Einhard, are seated at writing desks penning their histories of Charlemagne. Although it was regarded in the Middle Ages as the Archbishop's authentic account, the *Pseudo-Turpin* was in fact written *c.* 1140; it was very popular and frequently illustrated. Einhard was the contemporary and devoted servant of the Emperor and his history is full of circumstantial detail.

hood in arms. Two knights, not kinsmen, though they had probably been trained in the same household, would pledge themselves to each other as companions. Their pact was not necessarily formal, but it linked their fates as firmly as any feudal tie or even blood connection. The relationship would be recognized and respected by their fellows as a kind of warriors' marriage, for better or for worse. And in neither history nor legend do we find a more illustrious pair of companions than Roland and Oliver.

So by about 1100, when the *Song of Roland* as we know it was composed, France was emerging from its toils as a feudal monarchy, with all the political idealism and practical difficulties, all the possibilities of unity or internal rift and dislocation that implies. But what had been happening meanwhile to the Moslem order in Spain? The fierce ravagers of the Frankish coasts and borders had, by the tenth century, turned most of the Peninsula into a virtually independent state under the long-established Ummayad dynasty based in Cordoba. Here too, however, there were divisions and factions as well as the problem of the largely Christian lands in the north of the country.

Surprisingly, in view of their aggressive acts and their doctrine of the holy war, the Moslems showed much tolerance towards the many Christians and Jews in their own territories. As for their culture, they far outstripped the Franks in many spheres such as music, poetry, textiles, metalwork, ceramics and agriculture; and the French epics are strewn with references to Cordoban leather and the fine steel (as well as magic) of Toledo. French still carries words of Arabic derivation to remind us how much was owed in the Middle Ages to the skills and products of their civilization: among them figure the terms for algebra, alchemy, chess, lute, rebec, cotton, orange, sugar, and the humble spinach.

The eleventh century, however, saw Moslem Spain despite its flourishing culture cracked apart politically into feuding principalities; and whereas the petty Christian rulers of the north had not in the past been averse to appealing to the Saracens for support in their own quarrels, the situation was now reversed, and we find Moslems enlisting Christian aid. This state of affairs invited a more aggressive Christian policy; and in the later years of the eleventh century the Reconquest got well under way. The northern rulers pressed south against the Moslems, encouraged by the Church and especially by the militant monks of Cluny and with the active support of various Frankish nobles. In 1085 Toledo fell, and the papacy urged the faithful to carry through the struggle against the pagans in Spain. But in 1086 Berbers, summoned from Africa, advanced to stem the Christian tide. It was to be many years before the Reconquest was complete.

5 Charlemagne kneels, with Archbishop Turpin behind him, to present the Virgin with a model of the cathedral of Aix-la-Chapelle. The domed octagon of the chapel is clearly to be seen, and though the rest of the structure was altered, the interior of that part is much the same today (see also Plate 31).

6 The Christians are charging the Saracens, who flee, their ranks broken, to the right of the centrally placed horse. In a chapel (top right), Charlemagne is mourning his slain knights. These two panels are from the reliquary châsse of St. Charlemagne (see Plate 7).

7 Long side of the reliquary châsse of St. Charlemagne in Aix-la-Chapelle cathedral. This was completed in 1215, 50 years after the Emperor's canonization and 400 years after his death; it is only one of several reliquaries of the Emperor (*cf.* Plates 11–13). Silver-gilt repoussé panels on the roof illustrate the *Pseudo-Turpin Chronicle* (Plates 5, 6, 8, IV, 96) and statuettes of Charles's successors are ranged down the sides. On the end, Charlemagne himself is enthroned between Pope Leo III and Turpin. This work is a symbol of imperial dignity and a magnificent masterpiece of Mosan metalwork.

Already, however, the leaders of Christendom were turning their eyes elsewhere. By encouraging campaigns against the Spanish Saracens, the popes Alexander II and Gregory VII had helped to rouse a crusading spirit among the Frankish knights; and this fervour was now to be directed towards the liberation of Jerusalem and the Holy Places. In 1095 Pope Urban II, invoking the name and example of Charlemagne, called for an expedition against the infidels in the east; and it was established as an article of faith that all who died in the struggle would have their sins absolved and be received into Paradise. The Christian and pagan worlds were now in full collision. The First Crusade was launched. And about this time, it is thought, the *Roland*-poet composed his Song.

CHARLEMAGNE

'Our sovereign Charles, the mighty emperor'—so the Song begins, on a proud if nostalgic note. This is the glorious Charlemagne of legend, first and last to be mentioned, and whose presence, now luminous, now grim and dark as a thundercloud, broods over the entire Roland story. He is seen across the centuries as a majestic and venerable figure, walking at times close to God but at others with feet of all too human clay. But what can we say of the historical Charles, king of the Franks and only later emperor?

A man who served and knew him well was the scholar Einhard; and he has left a portrait which, though it may sometimes err on the side of flattery, contains many intimate details that have the flavour of truth. He cut a dignified figure, says Einhard, tall and strongly built, with a gay, good-humoured face and fine white hair. His eyes were large and piercing, his head domed and his nose a little on the long side. Despite a short, thick neck, a rather protruding stomach, and a voice less full than his physique promised, he always maintained an air of authority. He dressed in the Frankish style, with silk-edged tunic, long hose, shoes on his feet and cloth bands round his legs; against the winter cold he wore a fur jerkin, and he wrapped himself in a blue cloak. At his side he carried a gold- or silver-hilted sword, and a jewelled one on great state occasions. He enjoyed exercise, being not only a born horseman but a fine swimmer too. Indeed, it was because of his love of the thermal baths at Aix that he decided to build his palace there. However, in spite of all his vigour and activity, he was only a light sleeper and would wake four or five times during the night.

Plates 4, 80, 81

Behind the even temper and imperturbability mentioned by Einhard we glimpse a ruthless, unyielding will that would not brook opposition or offence. He would not be deterred by difficulties or danger; but his ends once achieved, he never let success go to his head. In many ways he showed

8 Charlemagne committed a sin so dreadful he dared not disclose it to his confessor St. Giles. Later while the Saint was saying Mass, it was revealed by an angel and Charles was absolved through the intercession of the Saint.

9 See p. 25. ▶

great generosity, lavishing gifts like those that so impressed the Irish kings of his day, or the great wealth that he sent to the pope in Rome. Indeed, the Church constantly benefited from his donations and endowments. Towards foreigners, says Einhard, he was particularly hospitable and magnanimous; and he was even on friendly terms with the Caliph of Baghdad, Harun-al-Rachid, who on one occasion presented him with an elephant. Messengers and gifts were exchanged with the Patriarch of Jerusalem (later legend credited Charles with having journeyed there himself), and also with successive Emperors of Constantinople. His contacts—and his vision—were truly international.

At the same time he seems to have been a dedicated family man. He took great care over the proper education and training of his sons and daughters, whom he took with him on all his journeys and retained within his household as long as he lived; except, that is, for two sons and a daughter who died before him. Their deaths, Einhard reports, 'he bore with less resignation than one would have expected from his strength of character; for his affection, no less strong, made him burst into tears'.

As befitted the lord of Christendom, Charles was extremely devout. He was a regular attender at morning Mass as well as the morning, evening and late-night hours; and as an enduring mark of his piety there was the rich chapel at Aix, for whose construction he had material brought from as far afield as Rome and Ravenna. Along with his devotion to religious matters went a keen interest in learning. Though he never himself mastered the art of writing, he spoke Latin fluently and even understood some Greek (his native tongue was, of course, the form of Germanic spoken by the Franks). Above all, he fostered a revival in education spearheaded by the Englishman Alcuin, who had been released from York to enter his service. At the same time, with his delight in good stories, he took steps to have the old heroic epics of the Franks committed to writing. It is a strange twist of fate that these should have perished, partly no doubt because they were overshadowed by the legend of Charlemagne himself.

Plates 5, 31

It would take long to detail the contributions made, directly or indirectly, by Charles to the arts and practical sciences. Einhard reserves special mention for his legal reforms and his architectural projects, the building of a great bridge over the Rhine and of palaces other than that at Aix, as well as the restoration of churches throughout his kingdom. Tribute is also paid to Charles's skill as a military tactician not only on land but in naval warfare too, for he built a fleet and strengthened the coastal defences against the Vikings and took similar measures against the Saracen marauders in the south. But even he was not entirely invincible; and Einhard gives a guarded account of that ill-starred expedition to Spain.

celluy temps estoiēt en cesarie deux roix sarrazins moult

10 In this woodcut, Ganelon on the left takes leave of Charles and on the right comes to plot treason with the two Kings of Saragossa, bearing the Emperor's message. The *Pseudo-Turpin* must be the ultimate source of this, as the *Song of Roland* speaks of only one King, Marsile (the second King is the Emir Baligant of the *Song*).

◄ 9 (Overleaf) Charlemagne institutes the Twelve Peers; to the right, his army marches back to France after the Spanish campaign. Above, the rearguard is ambushed by the heathen at Roncevaux.

11–12 These statues have been identified as Roland (left) and his companion-in-arms Oliver. The elder figure, Roland, has a lion rampant on his shield with its engrailed border, whereas the more youthful Oliver's emblem is a maiden. They stand sentinel with sword and lance, on the great Karlsreliquiar, made around 1360 to contain relics of Charlemagne.

In his seventy-second year, says his biographer, he was stricken down by pleurisy and buried amid much lamentation at Aix. Einhard speaks of the fearful portents that preceded his death: eclipses of sun and moon, a black spot seen for a week on the sun's face, earthquakes, a meteor, the collapse of a portico between chapel and palace, his bridge burnt, the beams of his chamber perpetually creaking, the roof of his basilica smitten by a thunderbolt, and inside, the inscription of his own name fading away. Charles, says Einhard, ignored these portents. For us they betoken the early beginnings of the Charlemagne legend.

We should not be surprised that the memory of a monarch called 'the Great' in his own lifetime should be increasingly magnified with the passing of the years. Monks heaped their superlatives on Charles in verse and prose; and more and more they told anecdotes of him that have the ring rather of popular tradition than of historical fact. Occasionally we come across features reminding us of things in the later epics: the king being warned in a dream of dire events, receiving one night from an angel an unsheathed sword, or shedding abundant tears at the thought of pagan Norsemen daring to attack his lands. And all the time the idea of the king-priest is gaining substance, the warrior apostle who spread the true faith in many lands either by the word or by the sword when the word failed, the Christian emperor who, as legend now asserts, made a pilgrimage to Jerusalem and brought back to France precious relics, including the Crown of Thorns, and a nail and fragment of wood from the True Cross. Such clerical encomiums and fictions as these bore fruit when, in 1165, Charlemagne was canonized at Aix-la-Chapelle.

Plate 6

Plate 7

Yet his legend was not all radiance and glory. According to an early tale, he once failed to pay his respects at a monastery, whereupon a tempest buffeted his boat on the Rhine until he had confessed his sins; then it abated. More sinister, within a decade of Charles's death a monk Wettin was transported in a vision to the Other World; and there, in Purgatory, was the Emperor suffering punishment for his sensuality when on earth, though destined eventually for the joys of Paradise. A later tradition, which was to affect the Roland story as we shall see, made much play of a certain secret sin of Charlemagne's. So grave was it that he did not dare mention it to the holy St. Giles; but at Mass an angel laid on the altar a document in which it was revealed, and Charles received absolution through the saint's intercession. It is unlikely that there was smoke without fire or that the Emperor's lustful reputation was mere slander. But it is time to turn back from moral to military failure.

Plate 8

III The battle of Roncevaux, from an early printed book made for Charles VIII. ▸

Puis que charlemaigne le trespu
issant empereur et tresrenomme
eut conquise toute galice & soubmise a la foy chrestiēne en lonneur de dieu
te de monseigneur saint iaques il retour-

na en france et fist ses osts heberger delez
pampelune. En ce tēps demouroiēt en la
cite de sarragoce deux roys sarrasis/ mar
cille & son frere baligāt. Si les auoit ēuoies
le soubdan de babilōne po: defēdre espaigne

13 Archbishop Turpin stands guard with Roland and Oliver (Plates 11–12) over the relics of Charlemagne. Turpin is represented as a prince of the Church and not the hard-hitting warrior of the *Song of Roland*.

RONCEVAUX

In the year 777 Charles had been successfully campaigning against the Saxons and was holding a great diet in Paderborn when a Saracen embassy arrived led by the governor of Barcelona, Suleiman Ibn Al-Arabí. The latter had rebelled with some confederates against the Emir of Cordoba, Abderrahman, and now invited Charles to give him support, promising in return their own loyalty and the submission of certain towns including Saragossa, on which the rebellion was centred. No doubt relishing this opportunity to extend Frankish and Christian influence in Spain, Charles, after spending the Easter of 778 in Aquitaine, assembled troops from various parts of his kingdom into a powerful army. In two columns it thrust into Spain, by the northern and southern routes. Charles himself led the northern column across the Pyrenees, and at Pamplona joined with Ibn Al-Arabí and received hostages from him. Thence he marched south to Saragossa to be met by his other column, which had come by way of Barcelona. But now he found that one of the Saracen rebels had laid hold of Saragossa and refused him entry. Instead of reducing the town by siege (perhaps he had received disturbing news from Saxony), he began his withdrawal to France, according to some accounts taking Ibn Al-Arabí with him. His return led him by way of Pamplona, whose walls he razed, and thence up through the passes of the Pyrenees.

None of the records written in Charles's lifetime tells us what happened then; but in the Royal Annals for the years to 829 grim events are related of which Einhard gives a fuller, more colourful description. He speaks of such successes as Charles had in Spain, then admits that his army's safe return through the Pyrenees was somewhat jeopardized by the perfidy of the Basques:

> For as his army proceeded, drawn out in a long file as dictated by the lie of the land and the narrow pass, the Basques had set on the crest of a mountain an ambush, to which the place lent itself because of the denseness of the woods, which are there at their thickest. They dashed down on the last section of the baggage train and the troops supporting the rearguard and shielding the main force that went ahead. These they forced down into the valley below, engaged them in battle, and slew them all to the last man. Then, having plundered the baggage, under cover of the falling darkness they scattered with utmost speed in all directions. In this exploit the Basques were helped by the lightness of their arms and the nature of the terrain where the engagement was fought; in contrast, the weight of their own arms and their disadvantageous position made the Franks no match for the Basques. In that battle were slain Eggihard, who was in charge of the royal table, Anshelm, Count of the Palace, and Roland, Lord of the Breton Marches, along with many another. And that action could not be avenged

Plate III

14 One of Roland's first feats of valour was to save his Emperor's life at Aspremont when he was menaced by the heathen Eaumont. By this deed he won his spurs as a knight.

15 The young Roland has recently been identified among the saints and martyrs at the south doorway at Chartres cathedral. He is shown as the Christian champion, the epitome of thirteenth-century chivalry, bearing in his right hand the standard of his Emperor, with on his shield the fleurs-de-lys of France.

on the spot since the enemy, having carried it out, dispersed so that nobody had the slightest idea where they might be sought.

This was the Battle of Roncevaux, as it has been known since the *Song of Roland*, and there is little that can be added. From the surviving epitaph of Eggihard the seneschal we know that it was fought on 15 August 778. Arabic sources claim Saracen participation and assert that Ibn Al-Arabí was rescued by his sons from Charles's grasp. But whatever the details, it is clear, as the royal annalist tells us, that the king lost many of his military leaders and made his way back to France with a heavy heart. It had certainly been a grave setback for him; and over sixty years after the event a writer could still say that he would refrain from mentioning the names of those slain with the rearguard since they were widely known. Legend may not be far short of the mark in recalling Roncevaux as Charles's greatest defeat.

But who was this Roland, *'Hruodlandus Brittannici limitis praefectus'*, one of the three Frankish victims singled out by Einhard? A man of some importance, it would seem, and surely the same Roland as figures prominently in a charter of about 772 among the nobles of the royal palace. Perhaps it is he too whose name stands in the abbreviated form 'Rodlan' on one face of a silver denier circulating before 790, while on the other we read the king's name, 'Carlus'. From now on, however, history remains silent; but the pages of legend begin to turn.

HISTORY INTO EPIC

Over three hundred years after so many Frankish warriors perished in the Pyrenean pass, a very remarkable man told of the disaster in song. Who he was we cannot say, only that the great poets of all time need feel no shame to have him in their company. His epic, called by later generations *The Song of Roland*, has been ranked with the first stained-glass window, the first Gothic arch, or the first troubadour lyric as one of those unexplained miracles of the Middle Ages. Yet it has only survived by the merest chance, in a nondescript little manuscript of the early twelfth century that can be seen today in Oxford's Bodleian Library.

The Oxford *Roland* is no versified chronicle or mere inflated account of the happenings of that August day in 778: it is a fully-fledged legend. Of the participants mentioned by Einhard, Charles is there, though prematurely given the dignity of emperor; and there too, of course, is Roland, *Plate 9* now become the king's beloved nephew and first of the twelve peers, Charles's faithful paladins. But of the other Christians and Saracens named in the poem, none is known to have been at Roncevaux: indeed most are either untraceable in history or else can be identified as belonging to a

16 The story of Roland's single combat with the giant Ferragut was a favourite with medieval illustrators. Here the Christians' champion is dealing the giant's death-blow in the navel, his one vulnerable spot.

IV This silver-gilt panel from the reliquary of St. Charlemagne (see Plate 7) shows a miracle: the lances of the knights to die in battle have burst into leaf. On the right of the tent in which Charlemagne is arming, the knights ride off to their martyrdom.

later period. There is no mention of the nominally Christian Basques who actually perpetrated the coup: the enemy is the Spanish King Marsile with his infidel hordes and then, in the later part of the poem, the Emir Baligant, summoned from Cairo to Marsile's aid. Moreover, the battle is no longer seen as a simple act of aggression and plunder, but as the dire outcome of a sinister plot hatched by one of the chief Christian lords, Count Ganelon, brother-in-law to Charles himself. As for the style of arms and equipment so vividly described by the poet, it would have been less familiar to Carolingian eyes than to the men of 1100; and the feudal institutions and ethics, the embryonic nationalism and the fervent crusading spirit, belong not to the eighth century but to the age of the First Crusade. How has all this come about? *Plate 10*

Scholars have long been interrogating the so-called 'silent centuries' between the event and the Song in the hope of answering this riddle. There is certainly evidence of the creative process of legend being early at work. One finds references in Latin texts to popular songs celebrating great men and events, and it is reasonable to suppose that these did not carry the truth unadorned. A fragment of Latin prose, probably of the early eleventh century, appears to summarize an epic account of the siege of a Saracen town by certain Christian heroes known otherwise from much later French poems. Even more interesting for us is the so-called *Nota Emilianense*, copied into a Spanish manuscript some time before 1070:

> In the year 778 King Charles came to Saragossa. At that time he had twelve nephews, each with three thousand knights in armour, among whom can be named Roland, Bertrand, Ogier Shortsword, William the Hook-nosed, Oliver and Bishop Turpin. Each of these, along with his followers, served the king for one month a year. It happened that the king stopped with his army in Saragossa. After a while, his men advised him to accept many gifts so that his army might not perish of hunger but return to their own land. This was done. Then it pleased the king that, for the safety of the men of his army, Roland the hardy warrior should form the rearguard with his men. But when the army crossed the pass of Cize, Roland was slain in Roncevaux by the Saracens.

So here, before the Oxford *Roland*, we find our hero in the company of his probably fictitious companion Oliver as well as of Turpin and figures familiar from other epics and we have, too, the place of the disaster named as Roncevaux. *Plates 11-13*

More intriguing still, William of Malmesbury wrote in 1125 that a song of Roland was struck up to put heart into the Normans at the Battle of Hastings in 1066. Now Gui de Ponthieu, who

17 An illustration from the Franco-Italian manuscript of *Les Enfances Roland* shows how, as a child, he took food from the table of Charlemagne for his parents.

died no more that eight years after the battle, had spoken of the inspiring words uttered there by a minstrel Taillefer. Though we are not told what those words were, we find in 1160 the French poet Wace combining the two pieces of information by saying that Taillefer had sung at Hastings of Charlemagne, Roland, Oliver, and the knights who died at Roncevaux.

What are we to conclude from such testimony, or from the fact that many years before the Oxford *Roland* was composed there appear in records more than one pair of brothers bearing the names of the two companions, Roland and Oliver? Surely that our legend had not been born overnight but had formed and developed over a wide span of years.

There is no need to go deeply into the lengthy debate over the origins of the *chanson de geste*, the French heroic epic. Scholars of an earlier generation believed that the poems we have (they can extend to 18,000 lines and more; the *Roland* has about 4,000) represent the final stage of a gradual process of growth, with short songs being composed soon after the events they recall and being fused as time passed to produce full-scale epics. This theory found a redoubtable opponent in Joseph Bédier, who believed them devised all of a piece from the late eleventh century onwards. They were, he thought, the result of co-operation between monks and minstrels plying the great pilgrim routes, where local heroic traditions would be gleaned and worked into epic form by individual poets. In the case of the *Roland,* Bédier believed the routes leading to the shrine at Santiago de Compostela to be of particular significance. Then the currents of scholarship shifted once more. Some recent critics have attached more importance to the influence of the Latin epics, classical or medieval, others to chronicle material, while others again have reverted to the idea of the oral transmission and gradual poetic elaboration of legends without interruption from the time of the events. Such new scraps of evidence as are brought to light certainly seem to support the theory of slow evolution. Yet one is loath to believe that the earliest of the poems we have, this magnificently wrought *Song of Roland*, is in its present form the work of many hands. Few would dispute that it bears the proud hallmark of a single artistic genius, even if he is to be thought of not as first creator but as ultimate redactor.

Although the *Roland* is the earliest and finest of the surviving *chansons de geste,* in other respects it stands as a typical example. To list their main features is not difficult. These tales of feudal and crusading strife were framed, of course, in verse, with the lines, usually of ten syllables, grouped into *laisses* or tirades of unequal length, each of which would carry the same assonance or, increasingly, rhyme. In the course of the twelfth and thirteenth centuries they tended to grow longer and more complex, largely under the influence of the romances, and many eventually found their way into massive prose compilations. But bald facts can never resurrect their true quality or that intense vitality that made them the staple of aristocratic and popular entertainment, at least until the rise of romance. This we can only try to conjure up in our imagination.

A jongleur, one of those wandering minstrels, arrives in a market place or castle hall with a new story to tell, or an old one dressed up afresh. He takes his vielle, a primitive fiddle, and perhaps strums a few notes; then, as the hubbub dies, he launches into his song. It may be that he sings to some recurring melody, or else in part recites his lines, reserving the musical delivery for certain passages of high suspense or pathos. But whether spoken or sung, the verse is full of music with its strong beat, assonance and occasional alliteration, repeated lines and phrases, verbal point and counterpoint, reappearing motifs and echoes of all kinds. The jongleur modulates his voice as he moves from council scene to battle-field or from speaker to speaker; his words ring with joy as the infidels bite the dust, groan out their news of a Christian hero's death. He pulls his audience into the situations he describes: 'Our mighty emperor . . .', 'See now the pagans . . .!', 'Had you but heard . . .!' Gesture and mimicry play their part in casting a spell over his hearers that will not be broken while the session lasts. Then perhaps he interrupts his tale to call for wine first and money after, and tomorrow he will be back to continue and conclude his song.

Because the jongleur needed to hold his public if he was not to starve, the poet (sometimes no doubt a minstrel himself) had to use every device at his command to grip and stimulate the imagination. The actual events of the story were not necessarily of first importance, for they might have been already well known. But the action had to be swift and taut, reality intensified and magnified. There was no time to be spent on analysis or the development of motives, for the live audience could not be asked to reflect on matters only to be overtaken by the fast-running narrative. Characters had to grow through their deeds and their reactions to the deeds of others. Dialogue, while a great boon to the oral performer, needed to be introduced in straightforward, easily remembered speeches.

This was true audio-visual art in the sense that while much of its impact came through the sounds of declamation and song and through the almost hypnotic rhythms and echoes of the verse, much too came from the presentation to the mind's eye of bright, easily focused images. With physical descriptions as with psychological, there was no room for indulgence. The call was for brilliant scenes painted in primary colours, statuesque attitudes, symbolic gestures and dramatic, stylized movements. The epics are full of dignified, white-bearded kings, of broad-shouldered, slim-waisted, blond, curly-haired heroes, of swarthy or deformed pagans, of red-headed traitors. Very often a single *laisse* will contain a complete, vividly evoked scene, neatly framed like the miniatures they inspired. As we look through the illustrations in this book, we may reflect

Map of Western Europe and the Kingdom of Charlemagne showing the places mentioned in the text.

18–19 These early sixteenth-century marquetry heads of Roland and Oliver have close similarities to a series of Bolognese niellos of the Nine Worthies. The medallions have been cut down and were probably originally inscribed ROLAND FILS MILON and OLIVIER DE VIENNE. They now decorate the choir-screen of the church of St. Bernard de Comminges and show the continued popularity of the heroes in the Renaissance.

that they represent an attempt to put on parchment or some other material, though with means so much less flexible than speech, the kind of pictures that would have flashed through the mind of an epic's audience as *laisse* succeeded *laisse.*

All these features, common to the *chansons de geste*, are present in rich measure in the *Song of Roland.* It has many other qualities besides, for instance an excellence of structure that rewards the closest analysis. The author has risen above the necessary conventions to which he was committed and has managed to convey a sense of his own involvement in the characters and their relationships. We are left with the impression of a deeply sensitive human being. But who was this man?

The true and simple answer is that we do not know. Yet even in our ignorance there is room for controversy. For the enigmatic last line of the poem contains a name that may or may not be his: Turoldus. Was this the author of the poem or its source? The copyist? Or a kind of editor who took the great man's work and dressed it up a little according to his own taste? For me, the latter possibility has the most to commend it. I believe, in fact, that Turoldus took the master's poem and expanded it by more than a third, chiefly by summoning a new figure, Baligant, to have a hand in the proceedings. The epic as he found it was truly the song of Roland: a story of betrayal, disaster and revenge, composed in three perfectly balanced movements and investigating feudal tensions and ideals within the context of a single campaign in a holy war. He widened its perspectives, confronting Charlemagne with the Emir of all Islam, adding a fourth movement and with it the spirit of Christendom on the march, the militant crusading fervour of his own day. It is hard to say who for him was the real hero—Roland or Charlemagne. Before his intervention there had been no doubt.

Plate 15

What are we to make of Roland? Was he the pure Christian warrior dedicated above all to the Cause, but doomed through treachery to die a martyr in the dark gorge of Roncevaux? Or was he too tainted with pride, so sure of his own strength that he overstepped the bounds of rightful conduct and had to expiate this fault of *démesure* before his soul was fit to be caught up by Gabriel into Paradise? Or was he the bold, valiant and dashing commander, admirable on the battle-field, but with a streak of pettiness and so vainly obsessed by his reputation that he was blind to the common good and to the welfare of those whose fates depended on him?

It was, I think, part of the master's achievement to see Roland from two angles at once: the poetic and the practical. He admired in him the image of the supreme feudal vassal, utterly committed to the triple ideal of duty to king and country, to family and to self, and prepared to pursue this ideal to the point where it claimed his own life. The master respected the military commander, earning his men's love by his unswerving example and his humble awareness of the ties of comradeship; his poetic vision was dazzled by Roland the warrior. But at the same time he viewed him through the steady eyes of the prudent companion Oliver, and felt at times with Ganelon the chafe of his overbearing arrogance. As poet on the one hand and moralist on the other, he conducted something of a love-hate relationship with his hero; and it is a highly complex portrait of Roland that he gives.

THE LATER ROLAND LEGENDS

The lack of early manuscripts other than the Oxford copy does not mean that this version of the *Song of Roland* was little known, even in the early years of the twelfth century. Its diffusion would have been largely by word of mouth: parchment was not cheap, and needy jongleurs would load their memories rather than their packs with the epic songs. In any case, it is plain that the Oxford manuscript itself does not carry the poet's lines without blemish, and so could not have been unique. There have survived various redactions in assonance or rhyme, but all copied considerably later than the Oxford text, and none so admirably concise. The tendency was to pad out the story with further action like Ganelon's escape from custody and re-arrest, or to dwell on existing incidents such as the sad fate of Roland's fiancée Aude, which touched courtly hearts grown tender from their exposure to sentimental romances.

The Church made a point of disparaging the vernacular heroic songs, which ran in competition with their own pious fictions. At the same time, the clerics were only too happy to make capital out of a suitable legend, and the Roland story won their favour. By about 1140 the *Pseudo-Turpin Chronicle* was produced, so called because it purported to be the true account of Charlemagne's Spanish campaigns given by the warrior archbishop himself, supposed to have survived Roncevaux, though still suffering a little from his wounds. The whole work is full of devout precepts and divine miracles. Surprisingly, perhaps, the apocalyptic battle with Baligant is omitted, though the Emir appears as King of Saragossa along with his brother Marsile. Less surprisingly, the fair Aude is given no role to play. However tedious the Chronicle may seem when set beside the Song, it was widely disseminated in the Middle Ages and greatly influenced the portrayal of our legend in art, as we shall discover. *Plate* IV

It is a common feature of the medieval epic that once a hero has made a name for himself in one poem, other stories are composed to fil out his fictional biography. So it was with Roland. First there was the matter of his parentage, of which the Song says nothing—out of tact, perhaps, for it may be that already the tradition regarding Charlemagne's secret sin was being linked (See *Plate 8*) with his nephew's name. This was done quite explicitly in a later Norse rendering of the legend: Charles committed incest with his sister Gisela but, when his lapse was made known to St. Giles, had the girl speedily married to Milo of Angers. Seven months later Roland was born. However, in another version the king's reputation is spared by making Roland the offspring of a secret liaison between Charles's sister and Milo; and the Franco-Italian poet who tells the tale even turns it to Roland's credit by contriving an analogy with the birth of Christ.

With our hero's birth and death accounted for, the legend-makers had a fairly free hand in inventing exploits to fill the years from his boyhood to that fine, fatal hour at Roncevaux. They simply had to make sure that his deeds were in character and did not run into conflict with the accepted facts of his uncle's campaigns. The *Song of Aspremont* is a good example of their efforts. Roland is still too young to bear arms, or so his uncle thinks. But with Charles off to do battle in Italy, the lad and some companions escape from their guardians and, on stolen horses, *Plate 14* follow him to Aspremont. There Roland slays the Saracen Eaumont and takes from him the sword Durendal. In recognition of the boy's spirit, Charles forthwith dubs him knight and girds Durendal at his side. Other texts in verse or prose multiply his adventures. How did he come to strike up a comradeship with Oliver? We are told this and learn, too, of the circumstances of his betrothal to Oliver's sister Aude. The manuscripts are studded with his feats of arms, including *Plate 16* the famous combat with the pagan giant Ferragut, already recounted in the *Pseudo-Turpin Chronicle*. We follow him with Charlemagne and his company to Jerusalem and on to Constantinople, where he threatens with a horn-blast to blow all the doors off the eastern Emperor's palace (a rare (See *Plate 108*) touch of humour in the French accounts of this most earnest knight) and we even see him journey to Persia and decline the hand of the Sultan's amorous daughter. Before the Middle Ages were out, Roland had been credited with a very full and active life.

His fame spread throughout Europe. Germany made much of him (if a little belatedly) as the nephew of that great man who was the very incarnation of the ideal of the Holy Roman Empire, cherished there above all in the twelfth century. A Bavarian priest, Conrad, translated (See *Plates 26*, V) the Song, intensifying its religious, crusading spirit; and in the thirteenth century his work was brought up to date by a Rhenish poet, Der Stricker. Wherever we turn we find evidence of the legend's popularity. There are versions in medieval Dutch and Welsh and despite the existence of a British Charlemagne in the person of King Arthur, a Middle English *Roland* was composed, the surviving text of which breaks off in mid-battle with the hero intent not on blowing his horn but on sending a messenger for help from Charles. It is only to be expected that Roland's memory was also preserved in the south of France, and a fragmentary Provençal poem on Roncevaux

20 Roland as the symbol of Imperial justice stands in the market-place of Dubrovnik. Such statues were popular in Germany in the fourteenth and fifteenth century, but this Yugoslavian example was erected to symbolize the town's defiance of Venice's claims of suzerainty.

V (Overleaf) Roland with Oliver at his side blows his horn and is heard by Charlemagne in a tower.

has come down to us. Nor was he forgotten south of the Pyrenees, though here he was soon to find in the shape of the gallant Cid (a historical figure of the late eleventh century) a rival in popular affection.

Plate 17

(See *Plate* 60)

It was the Italians in particular who took Roland to their hearts. As well as celebrating him in poems composed in dialects of Italian or Franco-Italian, they represented him in painting, sculpture (as in the well-known effigy which, with that of Oliver, flanks the doorway of Verona cathedral), and mosaic (scenes from the legend were set in the floor of Brindisi cathedral, only to be shattered by an earthquake in 1858). And his story lived on: at the end of the Middle Ages Luigi Pulci introduced a note of buffoonery into various episodes of his career, while in the vast *Orlando innamorato*, Boiardo made love the mainspring of his chivalry. Ariosto took up the subject where Boiardo had, for all his industry, left off. His *Orlando furioso*, full of marvels and fantasy (the hero's wits, for instance, leave him during a period of madness and are retrieved from the moon), further exploits the love theme but, despite its many remarkable qualities, continues to dissipate the primitive epic charge. With their delight in fantastic, sentimental adventure and their special gifts for burlesque and irony, the Italians had broadened Roland's experience, but reduced his stature.

We have come far from Einhard's simple account of what befell one August day in the passes of the Pyrenees. Perhaps we should be grateful to him and the early chroniclers for seeking to play down the gravity of the disaster, for by passing over it so quickly they provided legend with the space it needs to grow and flourish. So the Roland story gradually evolved, then spread far and wide, taking on more substance and new tonalities according to the various fashions of place and time. It did not die with the Middle Ages, but, given new impetus in the nineteenth century by the Romantics and in the field of scholarship by the discovery of the Oxford text, retains its honoured place in the European heritage and its great power to move us with pity and awe.

ROLAND IN ART

It is impossible to say when Roland first appears in art. Quite apart from the difficulties almost always present in the dating of medieval carvings, statues, manuscripts and the like, the craftsmen and artists could not be relied on to label their products clearly for posterity. Is this or that figure of a knight attacking his foe, Roland at grips with a Saracen, or is it perhaps an allegorical representation of virtue combating vice? This is the kind of question that must often go unanswered, and which even the most detailed recent studies cannot always settle. I shall offer here merely a few general observations on the nature of the legend's artistic legacy.

Als Rûlant swachet an siner stete und er do
sin horn so fast bliess das ym das hirn zerspielt
uff das es keiser Karle sin herre erhörte etc

V

21 The story of Roncevaux, painted by Simon Marmion. The priest saying Mass is Turpin and phases of the battle to come are being revealed to him in a divinely-sent vision (see also Plate 112).

ROLAND IN ART

The illustrations in this book show much of the range of materials and techniques that were put to the portrayal of Roland, though one might mention too his appearance in wall painting *Plates 18, 19* and enamel work, and even as the knave of diamonds on a sixteenth-century playing card. The Oxford manuscript did not rise to illustration. But what inspiration for the miniaturist there is in those dramatic scenes, many of them static, as if posed for the artist, with the characters holding their stylized attitudes and gestures! And the poet might almost have been instructing the painter as he called out the colours to be used: gold and silver, whites, yellows, blues, red against green. Yet the copies of what we may call the basic Roland legend do not really do it justice, with the honourable exception of the late thirteenth-century St. Gall manuscript of Der Stricker and its eleven richly worked pictures. Otherwise it is served principally by the thirty-nine capable and austerely elegant pen-drawings of the Heidelberg copy of Conrad's *Roland*, dated towards the end *Plate* V of the twelfth century, and the lively but impishly anachronistic pen and wash illustrations to Der Stricker probably executed by the Alsatian Diebolt Lauber about 1450. The more sumptuous miniatures are found in such secondary works as the *Entrée d'Espagne* or the various chronicles, *Plate* VI many of them by known artists like Loyset Liédet or Jean le Tavernier, whose painstaking grisailles bear the stamp of the professional workshop.

The work of the miniaturist is a major accomplishment, but for sheer luminous brilliance of hue, (See *Plates* what miniaturist could match the work of that artist in stained glass who has left us the famous XIII, XV) Roland window at Chartres? Its glowing scenes must have deflected the mind of many a worshipper from the priest's homily to muse on the glory and anguish of Christian chivalry in days long past. Beside them, how paltry and soulless seem the woodcuts, plain or painted, in the early printed accounts of our legend.

But printers, painters, workers in glass and stone, goldsmiths, silversmiths or weavers of tapestries all strove to communicate something of what the legend meant to them. So did the men who, in the fourteenth and fifteenth centuries, raised throughout the Empire, from Greifswald in the north to Dubrovnik in the south, colossal statues of its founder's mighty nephew, like so *Plate 20* many pillars lending it their support. This great Christian hero, sometimes (as at Chartres) represented with the halo of sainthood, never quite aspired to the heights of official canonization like his uncle; but is there not in those gigantic statues something of the tutelary deity watching over the destiny of Charlemagne's former realm?

How lonely the statues look now as they stand amid the busy city streets. Robbed of their context, they are left isolated in time and place. This is a far cry from the art of the miniaturist, who seldom portrayed the single figure, preferring the crowded court or battle scenes, where it is

Rolant

22–23 Roland cleaves Marsile in two in the confused violence of battle shown on a Tournai tapestry. Ganelon enumerates the terms proposed by Charlemagne to the Kings of Saragossa. The slaying of Marsile at Roncevaux and the co-rulers are elements from the popular *Pseudo-Turpin Chronicle* which do not occur in the *Chanson de Roland*.

often only the gilded helmet or the shield blazoned with fleurs-de-lys that enables us to pick out Roland from the throng. Not only did they like to fill their allotted area of parchment with the numerous details of a particular scene, but they frequently managed to illustrate several quite different episodes within the single frame. Thus Simon Marmion, embellishing a manuscript of *Plate 21* the *Grandes Chroniques de France*, shows us not only the Battle of Roncevaux but also Ganelon's treason, his death and that of Roland, and Archbishop Turpin having his vision, all in a single *Plate 22* picture. The Roncevaux tapestries are packed with incident upon incident to the point of confusion. Other artists, like the splendid illustrator of the St. Gall manuscript, chose to group scenes together, but separated from each other by a border. Another technique, employed in the Heidelberg manuscript of Conrad's poem, is to represent each important event at its proper place in the text. But one man, the illustrator of the Venice *Entrée d'Espagne*, went even further by (See *Plate 27*) following every development in his story with pictures that serve like successive frames in a film to carry the action along. In our next section we have tried as far as possible to emulate this early exponent of the strip cartoon by selecting and arranging illustrations so as to form a pictorial commentary on the *Song of Roland*, retold from the Oxford version.

Some details of the pictures, it will be found, conflict with our telling of the story. This is because, as I have said, that form of the legend was never lavishly treated by the miniaturists. *Plates 23*, VII In fact the most influential text as far as the later accounts of Roncevaux are concerned was the *Pseudo-Turpin Chronicle*, with its two kings of Saragossa, its slaying rather than maiming of Marsile, the appearance of Roland's half-brother Baldwin as the hero lay dying, Turpin's vision (See *Plate 111*) and many other divergent elements. It was this same Chronicle that popularized whole episodes foreign to the Oxford text, the most striking example being Roland's fight with Ferragut, upon which the artists seized with quite remarkable enthusiasm. Some of these we shall consider in the last section of the book.

As we turn now to the stories themselves and follow the great happenings through the pictures, we may reflect on the service those medieval artists have performed for the legend. It was beyond their power to translate in pictorial terms the swift thrust and vigour of the Song; for ink, paint and chisel are so much less supple than the living word. They could not convey the nuances of tenderness or remorse or dark insinuation that we find in the verse. They had to simplify the action and leave its motivation unstated. But what they could and did achieve through *Plate 24* the expressive placing and gestures of their figures, was to portray the public face of that heroic ideal of militant Christianity which the poet had sung, in travail and disaster, but ultimately in triumph.

VI Charlemagne, wearing the blue and gold of the French Royal House, receives the hostages and camels laden with gifts from Saragossa. On the right, Roland attacks Marsile and strikes off his right arm, as recounted in the *Song of Roland* (see Plates 22, VII).

24 These superb statues in Rheims cathedral have been identified as Turpin giving communion to Roland before battle. Roland is clad in chain mail from head to toe, in thirteenth-century style. Behind him, Marsile glowers in the shadows, wearing Saracen armour. Turpin was Archbishop of Rheims and it is thus fitting he should be shown here administering the rites of the Church to one who was to become a Christian martyr.

VII (Overleaf) With a mighty blow of his sword, Roland cuts Marsile clean in two. Below, Roland lies stiff in death, Durendal at his feet. ▶

tuez tous les combatans qui la estoiet
des noz fors Rollant baudouyn et thierri
Car turpin et guenelon estoient avecques
le Roy

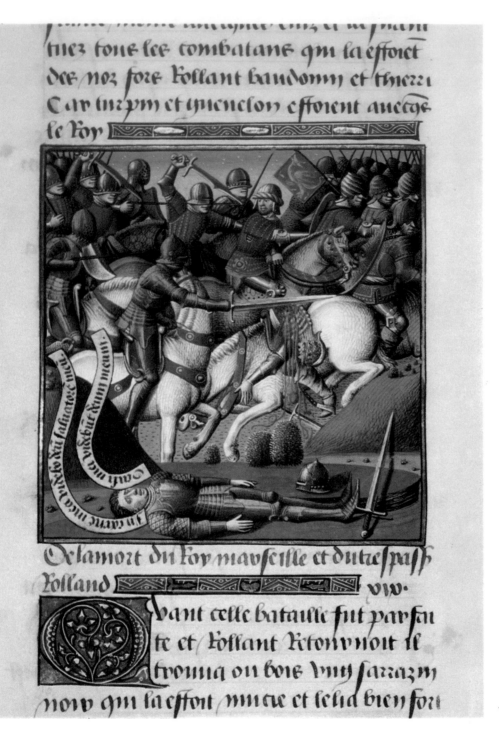

De la mort du Roy marseille et du trespas de
Rolland .viii.

Quant celle bataille fut parfai
te et Rollant retournoit il
trouva ou bois vng sarrazin
noir qui la estoit mucie et se lia bien fort

VII

The Song of Roland

CHARLES OUR MIGHTY EMPEROR, so the Song begins, has warred in Spain for seven years and conquered the whole land except for Saragossa on its mountain top. There rules King Marsile, God's enemy. But for him a grim fate is in store.

In Saragossa there is a shady garden, where Marsile reclines among the highest of his lords. He asks their counsel: what must they do to rid themselves of Charles? Only the wise and trusty Blancandrin of Castel del Valfunde replies: 'Offer him rich gifts—gold and silver, lions, bears, camels, hawks and hounds. Promise him then your service and acceptance of the Christian faith on condition that he withdraw to France and Aix. Say you will follow him there at Michaelmas. If he wants hostages, send them: better that our sons lose their heads than that we surrender all our territories. Then you'll see the Frankish army disband at once. At Michaelmas Charles will await our coming in his great chapel at Aix; and when there is no word of us, our hostages will perish—but our fair land of Spain will be saved.'

The treacherous plan is approved. Marsile calls upon Blancandrin to go with nine others to Charlemagne, who is laying siege to Cordoba. They are to bear olive branches as a token of peace and humility; and if they can achieve the pact, they will be well rewarded. On ten white mules the messengers set out with their olive branches in their hands, but deceit in their hearts.

Now the scene switches to the jubilant Charlemagne, who has just seized Cordoba with rich booty, slaying or converting all its infidel defenders. In a garden there, under a pine and beside *Plate 25* a wild rose tree, the Emperor sits on a golden throne, a striking figure with his fine white hair and beard, and his proud, noble bearing. At his side are Roland, Oliver and many other of his *Plate 26* barons. Nearby, knights rest on silken cloths, some playing backgammon and the older ones chess, while younger men try their skill at fencing. This is the sight that meets the eyes of the heathen messengers when they arrive.

25 The typical aftermath of a Frankish victory in the Spanish war: a pagan in a phrygian cap, always the distinguishing mark of the heathen, kneels before an idol. In the centre, Roland resolutely slices an idol in two; behind him lie the bodies of the newly-slain Moors, their naked souls being taken by black demons above. Turpin baptizes the new Christians who stand in attitudes of prayer in a large font. Behind them are their sponsors, and, at the back of the crowd, Charlemagne. As the *Song* puts it, with crushing simplicity:

> 'All pagans in the city have been slain,
> Or else converted to the Christian faith.'
> (ll. 101–2)

26 Seated on his throne, the Emperor with his long white beard turns to his sword-bearer Roland:

> 'In a great garden there the Emperor
> Has at his side Roland and Oliver.'
>
> (ll. 103–4)

Also wonete do da. der keiser in yspania. vil har
te gwaldecliche. in allem dem riche. dorf un̄
burige. hereter al garwe. turne un̄ mure , veste

Plates 27, 28 They dismount from their mules and greet the Emperor with feigned affection. When Blancandrin, as spokesman, has briefly put their proposals, Charlemagne raises his hands to God, then bows his head in thought. When at length he looks up, his face is full of fierce pride: 'Your words are fair, but how can I trust them when Marsile is my sworn enemy?'—'You'll have hostages,' replies Blancandrin, 'and my own son among them. Then my lord will follow you to Aix and in your baths there take the Christian faith at St. Michael's feast.'—'Then he may yet be saved,' says Charles. That night the messengers are well lodged and attended.

In the morning the Emperor rises early to attend Matins and Mass, then takes his place beneath *Plate 29* a pine and calls his Franks to council, for on their advice he places his whole reliance. More than a thousand assemble; and with them come Roland, his companion Oliver, and Ganelon who, says the poet, wrought the treachery. So the ill-fated council begins, with Charles putting the terms proposed by Marsile, but expressing his own doubt as to the pagans' purpose. The French too are wary.

In Roland's mind, however, no doubt exists: 'Never believe Marsile! We came to Spain seven *Plate* VIII years ago, and I have conquered much of it for you. But when I took Seville the pagan king sent messengers, all bearing olive branches and offering these same terms. The Franks then advised you ill. You sent him two of your counts, Basan and Basile; and in the hills by Haltile he cut off their heads. Carry on with the war! March on Saragossa and, if need be, besiege it all your life and avenge the slaying of your men!' Charles sits with lowered eyes, silently stroking his moustache and beard.

At this, Ganelon steps proudly forward: 'Put no trust in rogues! When Marsile offers to become your vassal, holding Spain as his fief, whoever speaks against these terms holds our lives cheap. Let us be guided by wisdom, not foolishness'. Duke Naimes supports Ganelon: 'Marsile is beaten, and you should show him mercy'. With this the Franks concur, and that is enough for Charles: 'Whom then shall we send to Saragossa to treat with him?' Naimes himself offers but is told to sit down by the king, who needs the services of his wise counsellor. At once Roland volunteers. 'No', says Oliver, 'you're too rash and violent for the task. But I'll go, if the king wishes'.—'Be quiet, both of you!' Charles exclaims. 'Neither you nor any of my twelve peers shall go'. The French are shocked by the curt veto; but the king proceeds to reject Archbishop Turpin's offer too.

We may wonder if, despite his obvious reluctance to let any of his favoured men undertake so dangerous a mission, Charles is not technically in the right: he had asked for a nomination, and so far only volunteers have come forward. In any case, he calls the Franks once more to make

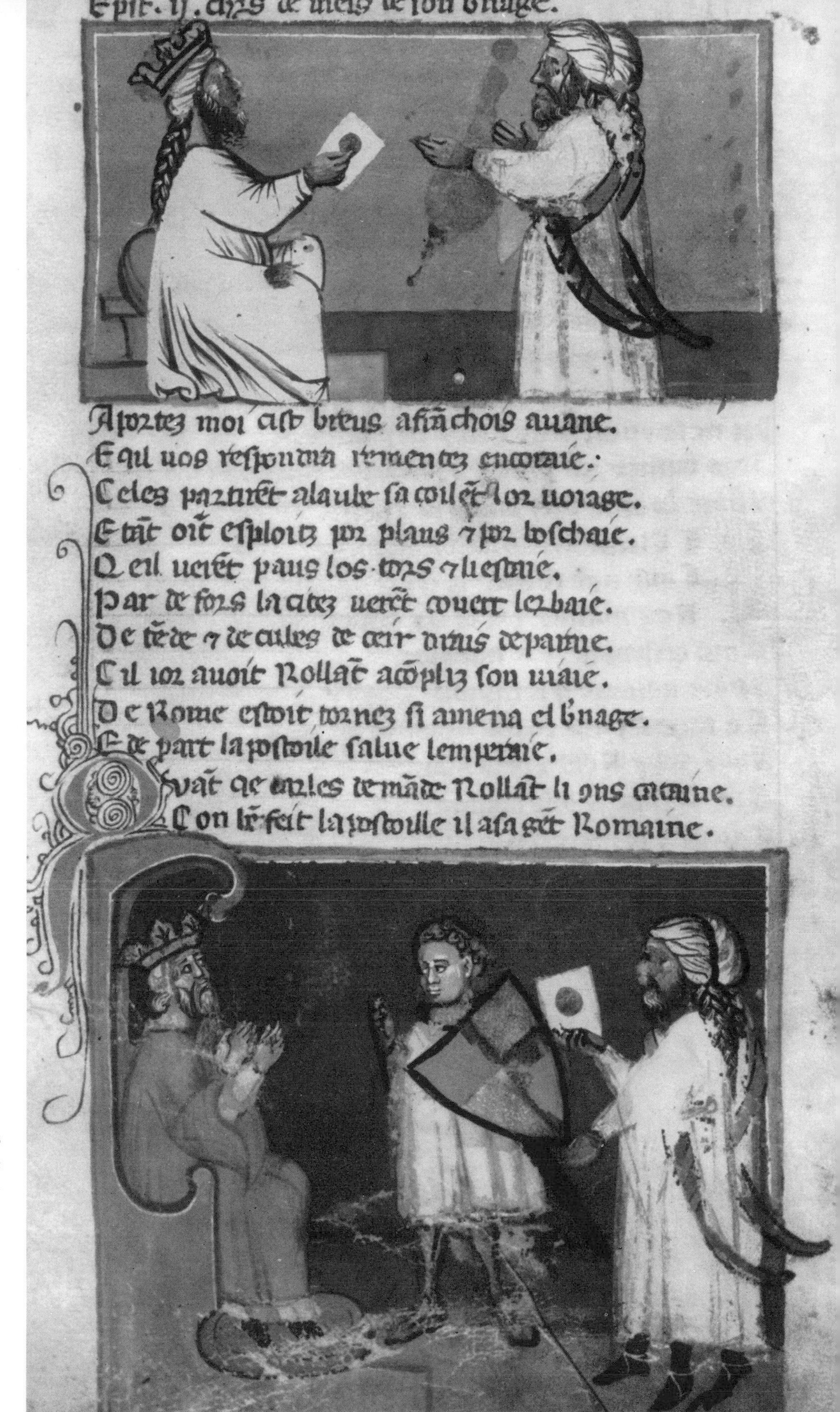

27 The heathen messengers are handed a letter by Marsile and below, deliver it to Charlemagne as Roland looks on.

VIII High on a hill, Roland points out the city of Noples; the gates are stormed. This was one of Roland's conquests in the seven-year Spanish campaign.

a choice. Roland reacts with typical promptness, but with fatal consequences: 'Send my stepfather Ganelon.'—'Yes', say the French, 'you couldn't send a wiser man'. Ganelon's response testifies to a bitterness that already exists between the two men. Leaping to his feet, he flings off his fur cloak, impressively handsome with his eyes flashing in his proud face: 'Fool, what madness is this? Everyone knows I'm your stepfather, yet you propose that I go to Marsile. If God grant that I return, I'll start a lifelong feud with you!'—'What stupid arrogance!' jeers Roland. 'Still, this is a job for a wise man: I'll go in your place, if the King agrees.'—'Never!' Ganelon snaps. 'I'll go to Saragossa for Charles; but I'll do something rash before my anger cools.' When Roland hears this, he begins to laugh. Bursting with rage, Ganelon spits out his hatred for his stepson, who has falsely nominated him; but then he places himself at the Emperor's command. *Plate 30*

'I know I must go to Saragossa and will not return', he says to Charles. 'My wife is your sister, and Baldwin our son will be a fine man. Protect him well: I'll not see him again'. The King replies: 'You're too soft-hearted. You must obey me and depart. Take now this glove and staff of office: the Franks have chosen you.'—'Sire, Roland brought this about. Here in your presence I defy him, and Oliver since he's his companion, and the twelve peers since they love him so!'—'You're too full of rage', says the King and again bids him go, handing him his right glove. But when Ganelon goes to take it, the glove falls; and the Franks are apprehensive, seeing here an ill omen. 'You'll hear more of this!' Ganelon declares. 'Give me my leave now, sire.'—'Go, in Christ's name and in mine.' Charles signs him with the cross, then hands him the staff and the letter for Marsile. *Plate 32*

Ganelon goes straight to his lodging to make ready for the journey. With golden spurs at his heels and his sword Murgleis at his side, he mounts Tachebrun his horse while his uncle holds the stirrup. His comrades weep and speak of vengeance against Roland. They ask to go with him; but Ganelon proudly declares that rather than take them to their deaths he would die alone. Asking them to bear his greetings to his wife, his dear friend Pinabel, and Baldwin his son, he takes the road for Saragossa.

He comes up with the pagan messengers, and Blancandrin rides with him behind the rest. 'Charles is a wonderful man,' says the infidel: 'he has conquered Apulia and Calabria, and crossed to England to obtain St. Peter's dues. But what does he want of us?'—'No one can vie with him,' Ganelon replies.—'He's ill advised by his barons'.—'By none but Roland; and he'll pay for it one day. Yesterday morning he came fresh from plundering by Carcassonne to hand his uncle a crimson apple. "Here," he said, "I offer you the crown of all the kings." But every day he toys with death; and if someone should slay him, his arrogance would have its reward, and we should find

Also der bischoff mit eime grossen volck für den
keiser trat/ vnd den herren ire rede det/

28–29 (Left) Charles stood outside his tent and

> 'The messengers dismounted from their mules
> To greet him warmly with a show of love.' (ll. 120–1)

Having heard their message,

> 'The Emperor has gone beneath a pine
> And, to conclude his council, called his lords.' (ll. 168–9)

The manuscript of *Karl der Grosse* illustrates the early stages of the Roland story in detail, though its style lacks variety.

30 (Below) The peers agree on Ganelon as emissary; he is unwilling but Charles insists: 'Since I command it, you must needs depart!' (l. 318)

31 The west front of the Palace Chapel at Aix-la-Chapelle, built by Charlemagne on the plan of S. Vitale in Ravenna. The tower above is Gothic, but the great niche above the main entrance is a Carolingian feature. Charles used to stand there to address his people. A model of the whole church as it was originally conceived is held by the Emperor on the reliquary of St. Charlemagne (above, Plate 5).

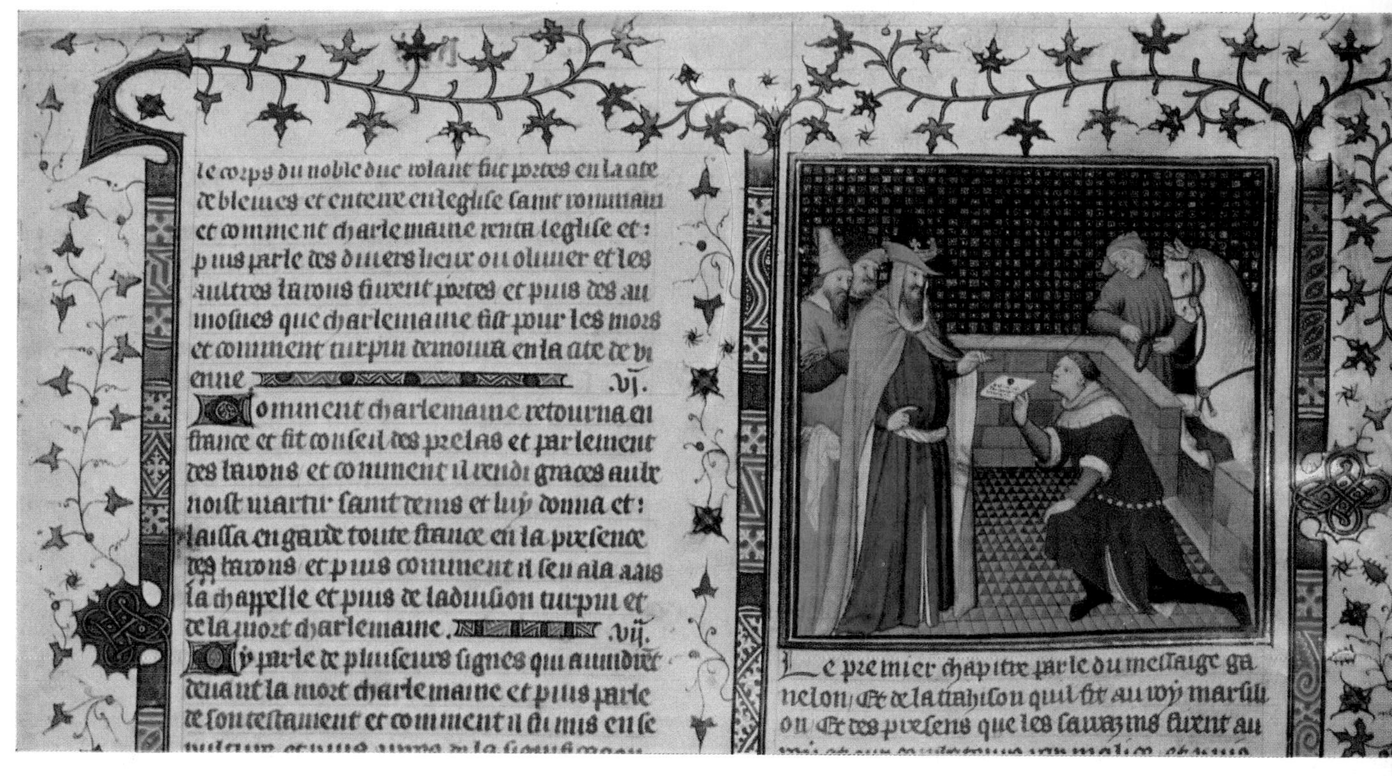

IX Ganelon delivers Charlemagne's message to Marsile: 'Here is the letter from our Emperor.' (l.483) Two councillors stand behind the evil-looking King. Ganelon has left his horse with a groom and kneels before Marsile, offering the document with its royal seal. This manuscript of the *Grandes Chroniques de France* may have been made for that magnificent art patron, John, Duke of Berry. As the French Royal House traced its ancestry from Charlemagne, the Roland story often appears in the Chronicles.

peace.' So they talk together, with Ganelon telling the Saracen of the Franks' great love for Roland because of the wealth he has bestowed on them, while to him the Emperor owes his

Plate 33 whole dominion. And before they arrive in Saragossa, they have vowed together to try to bring about Roland's death.

In his city Marsile and the pagans wait for news. The king is sitting in the shade of a pine on a throne draped with Alexandrian silk when Blancandrin appears, leading Count Ganelon by the hand. This man, he says, will give Charlemagne's reply. Choosing his words with care, Ganelon first greets Marsile, then announces what the Emperor demands of him: that he should receive the Christian faith and afterwards hold half of Spain as his fief. Failing this, he will be taken in chains to Aix for final judgement and execution. In his alarm, all colour drains from Marsile's face. He catches up a javelin and brandishes it. Ganelon's hand goes to his sword; and as he begins to draw it from the scabbard, he addresses it, vowing not to yield up his life before the best in this foreign land have paid its price. But the pagans restrain Marsile, and he listens enraged as Ganelon repeats the terms, adding now that Spain will be shared between him and

Plate IX Roland. With that the Frenchman hands over Charlemagne's letter; but it gives Marsile no comfort, for it contains yet another requirement: that he must surrender his own uncle, the Caliph Ganelon, when the king's son calls for his death, sets his back to the pine, his drawn sword in his hand.

But now Marsile withdraws into his garden with his son, his uncle, and Blancandrin, who assures him that Ganelon has pledged to act to their advantage. Marsile, his wrath abated, has the Count brought again into his presence. Apologizing for his rashness in almost striking him, he gives him rich sable furs and promises more wealth before the next day is out. Ganelon graciously

Plate 34 accepts the gift. Then he is asked to speak of Charlemagne. He is more than two hundred years old, the pagan believes: when will he ever give up his campaigning? Ganelon speaks out in praise of the Emperor's great nobility.—But when will he cease his campaigns?—Never, so long as Roland lives, a knight unmatched on earth, who forms his vanguard with Oliver and the twelve peers and twenty thousand knights to give Charles complete security.

'I can command four hundred thousand men', says the king. 'With them can I engage Charles and the Franks?—'You must bide your time', Ganelon replies. 'Send him much wealth and twenty hostages. Then he will turn back to fair France, leaving behind his rearguard; and there, I think, will be Roland and Oliver. Then, if you take my advice, the counts will perish, and with them Charles's pride. Never again will he make war on you.'—'But how can this be done?'—'I'll tell you. The king will be at the main pass of Cize, his rearguard left with Roland, Oliver, and twenty thousand Franks. First send against them a hundred thousand of your Saracens. There will be

32 'The Emperor then hands him his right glove.
Count Ganelon wished he were far away,
And when he went to take it, the glove fell.'
(ll. 331–3)

The dropped glove can be seen between Ganelon and Charles, a detail not shown in other manuscripts. At the Emperor's side stands his nephew and sword-bearer, Roland, Ganelon's stepson. The name 'Genelun' has been inscribed over the traitor's head by a twelfth-century reader. The Bavarian *Ruolantes Liet* is the earliest manuscript of the Roland story with illustrations, and in many details it is close to the Oxford text. The translation was made around 1180 by Conrad the Priest for Henry the Lion, Duke of Bavaria, whose wife was French.

le roy charle le tyrant sachās
ces .ij. rois estre en ceste cite lez
manda par lun de ses princes
nommez ganelon ou que ilz re

chargies de tresbon vin pur et
doulx pour boire z enyvrer les
combatans du roy charle. z si
envoyerent en lost des yviens

33 The traitor sets out on his mission to Saragossa:

'Ganelon rode beneath tall olive trees
And joined up with the pagan messengers.'
(ll. 366–7)

◂ X Ganelon's return with the fateful gifts from Saragossa.

Comment la trahison de raincheuaulx fu com
pilee accordee et bastie par marcille de sarragoce
et guennelon le conte des pays de champaigne

34–35 Ganelon and Marsile plot the downfall of Roland (opposite)

> ' "Worthy Sir Ganelon," said King Marsile,
> "In what way can I compass Roland's death?" '
> (ll. 580–1)

Ganelon revealed his plan, and king and traitor then swore faith on Marsile's idol.

> 'Thus spoke Marsile, "Why should we parley more?
> Roland's betrayal you should pledge to me."
> And Ganelon replied: "Just as you will." '
> (ll. 603, 605–6)

great loss on both sides; but then join battle again. Roland will not survive both these encounters, and you'll have gained your freedom. With him Charles will have lost his own right arm and will never gather such might again. In this way we shall all have peace.' Marsile kisses Ganelon on
Plate 37 his cheek; and then they begin to bring the treasure out.

'Why waste more words?' says the pagan. 'Pledge me the betrayal of Roland.' On the relics in
Plates 35, 36 the hilt of his sword Murgleis Ganelon swears the treason and succumbs to sin. Seated on a throne of ivory, Marsile orders that a book of his gods' law be brought; and in his turn he takes an oath to attack Roland in the rearguard and bring him to his end. 'So be it,' says Ganelon.

A pagan, Valdabrun, steps forward with a laugh to offer the Count his priceless sword, if he will promise that they will find Roland in the rearguard. 'It shall be done', Ganelon says; and they exchange embraces. Another infidel, Climborin, bestows his fine helmet in similar fashion. And after him comes Bramimonde the Queen: 'Since my lord and his men hold you in such esteem, you have my affection too. Here are two necklaces heavy with gold, jacinths and amethysts: take them for your wife.' These also Ganelon accepts. Marsile asks his treasurer if the tribute for Charles is prepared. Seven hundred camel-loads of silver and gold are there, and the twenty hostages too. The king takes Ganelon by the shoulder: 'Keep faith with us, and you shall have ten mules laden with gold, now and every year. Here, take this city's keys and its wealth to Charles. Then name Roland to the rearguard for me so I may battle with him to the death.'—
Plate 38 'I wait here too long,' says Ganelon. Mounting, he begins the journey back.

The Emperor has started his withdrawal. At the citadel of Galne, laid waste by Roland, he awaits news of his messenger. In the early morning after his devotions he stands by his tent with
Plates 39, 40, X, XI Roland, Oliver, Duke Naimes and many others, when Ganelon arrives and greets him: 'God save you, sire! From Saragossa I bring the keys, and with them vast wealth and twenty hostages. Marsile would have sent his uncle the Caliph; but with my own eyes I saw him flee with four hundred thousand armed men who refused to take the Christian faith. They took to the sea, but only to be caught by a tempest and drowned, every one. The king himself, though, will do all you ask.'—'Praise be to God!' exclaims Charlemagne. 'You shall be well rewarded.' Bugles resound through the army. The Franks assemble and strike camp; then they take the road towards fair France.

Plate 41 The day passes, and Roland mounts a hill where, binding the standard to his lance, he raises it against the sky. The army bivouacks in the countryside, not knowing that through the valleys the pagans ride with swords girt and lances decked. At nightfall the heathen troops halt in a wood high up in the hills.

36 To make his oath to betray Roland more binding, Marsile has Ganelon swear on his own sword:

> 'Upon the relics of his sword Murgleis
> He swore the treason and succumbed to sin.'
>
> (ll. 607–8)

37 The destruction of Roland having been plotted, gifts are prepared for Charlemagne and brought before Marsile for his approval.

As Charles lies sleeping, he dreams that he is in the pass of Cize when Ganelon seizes his lance and brandishes it with such violence that it flies in splinters to the sky. Again he dreams: he is at his chapel in Aix, when a ferocious bear bites his right arm, and he is fiercely attacked by a leopard come from Spain. Out of his hall leaps a hound that rips off the bear's right ear and launches itself upon the leopard. The Franks cannot tell how the contest will end. For a third time Charles dreams: at Aix he holds a bear in fetters, when thirty others come from the Ardennes to call in human voices for their kinsman's release. From the palace there runs a hound that falls upon the biggest of the bears; but the King cannot tell which will get the upper hand. He does not wake until the bright day dawns. *Plate 42*

Next day he mounts to ride with his men. 'Here are the passes,' he calls: 'appoint for me now the leader of the rearguard!'—'My stepson Roland', is Ganelon's prompt reply: 'you have no baron as valiant as he.' Charles is filled with wrath: 'You are a living fiend from Hell!' But he does not question the nomination. 'Who then shall lead in the van?' Ganelon proposes Ogier of Denmark. Roland does not hesitate to accept the post. Proudly he assures the Emperor that he will suffer no loss that is not first paid for by the sword, a fact freely acknowledged by Ganelon. But then he rounds on his stepfather: 'Did you think I'd let the glove fall to the ground like you?' He calls for the bow as token of his command. Charles bends his head, and tears fill his eyes. But at Naimes' prompting he confirms the appointment, then urges his nephew to keep half the army as protection. 'I'll do no such thing!' Roland scornfully retorts. 'God curse me, if I let my family down! I'll take twenty thousand Franks, and you can cross through the passes without fear.' Oliver and other peers are quick to rally to him. Gautier de l'Hum he orders to patrol the defiles and the heights. The stage is set for the bitter battle to come. *Plate 43* *Plate 44*

(We may pause here to reflect on the sowing of the seeds of treachery and their germination. Has Roland, the great champion of Christendom, been betrayed by a double-dyed villain warped by jealousy and greed? Has he been betrayed at all, when he and his comrades had been openly defied? Or are we to think of him reaping the reward of his self-centred arrogance and cold disregard of the feelings of more ordinary mortals? Has Roland's loyalty to Charlemagne appeared more plainly than Ganelon's? Has the Emperor himself been as impartial and fair-minded as he should be? These questions will be with us until the end of the Song.)

The hills are high, the valleys plunged in shadow. Charles and the army after a day's march are in sight of Gascony and their fatherland. They think of their wives and the maidens there; and they weep, the King most bitterly of all, to have left Roland in the Spanish pass. Though the twelve peers there have no fear of death, Charles hides his grief beneath his cloak, for, as he

Cy parle du messaige ganelon et de la
traÿson quil fist au roy marsilion et
des presens que les sarrazins firent
au roy charlemaine et aux contes
par malice.
Puis que charlemaine
le trespuissant empereur
et tres renomme ot ac
quise toute galice et
soubmise a la foy crestien
enne a lonneur de dieu
et de monseigneur sait
iasque il retourna en

38 This version of events shows the Kings of Saragossa accompanying Marsile with laden horses.

reveals to Naimes, an angel has warned him in a dream that France will be destroyed by Ganelon; and he it was who named Roland for the rearguard. All there feel grief for Charlemagne and dread for his nephew's fate.

In Saragossa Marsile has summoned his men, sounded his drums, raised up Mahomet to the highest tower and worshipped him. And then his host ride through Cerdaña's hills and vales until they can see the Frankish banners. It is the rearguard, who will not flinch when the battle is joined. Astride a mule, Marsile's nephew Aelroth thrusts forward before the king to claim the first blow against Roland, and Marsile grants the request by handing him a glove; whereupon Aelroth calls for twelve of the highest pagan lords to fight with him against the peers. Falsaron, Marsile's brother, is the first to reply; and he is joined by Corsablis a Berber king, Malprimis of Brigant, the gallant and handsome Emir of Balaguer, an almanzor of Moriane, Count Turgis of Turtelose, and Escremis of Valterne, all vowing vengeance on Roland and the companions. At the King's bidding, Estorgans and his comrade Estramariz join them, pledging to hand over to him Charlemagne himself. Then Margariz of Seville comes forward, an infidel so chivalrous and good-looking that all the Saracen ladies dote on him and welcome him with laughter everywhere. His boast is that within a year they will be lodging in France at Saint-Denis. Lastly comes Chernuble of Munigre, a Saracen of immense strength, whose long hair sweeps the ground. His sunless land, it is said, has never seen rain or dew, and no grain grows among its pitch-black stones: some declare it is the haunt of fiends. He makes his boast; and then all twelve pagan peers go to a pine wood to don their arms, along with a hundred thousand infidels.

They put on their mailed hauberks, lace their helms, gird their swords of Viana steel, and take up their shields and lances, where crimson, blue and white pennants flutter. Leaving their palfreys and mules, they mount their war-steeds. Their equipment glitters in the sun, while a thousand bugles sound forth a flourish. The Frenchmen hear the clamour. Oliver says: 'Companion, we may do battle with the Saracens.'—'May God grant it so!' replies Roland. 'It's our duty to stand firm for our King: a man should be ready to suffer great hardship for his lord. Let us all strike mighty blows so no one can sing a mocking song of us! Pagans are wrong and Christians in the right! I'll set no bad example.'

From a hilltop Oliver spies the gleam of pagan arms and reports their vast number. 'The traitor Ganelon knew something of this when he nominated us before the Emperor.'—'Say no more, Oliver!' Roland retorts. 'You speak of my stepfather.' Oliver hurries from the hill to warn the rest of the Frenchmen of the approaching hordes. He tells them they will see such a battle as never before: they must hold fast. 'For you we'll do our duty to the death,' is their reply. *Plate 46*

He calls again to Roland: 'Now sound your horn so that Charles will hear and turn his army back!' His companion refuses: 'Should I act like a fool and lose my reputation in fair France? No: I shall strike great blows with Durendal, and the pagans' blood shall stain its blade to the golden hilt. They are all marked for death.' Oliver repeats his plea, and makes it a third time; the reply is still the same. 'But there's no blame in this', he says. 'I've seen the Saracens swarming over every hill and valley. Our men are so few beside them.'—'That's how I like it,' says Roland. 'The greater our blows, the more dearly the Emperor loves us.'

Roland is valiant, Oliver is wise. They are two matchless knights, and together they face the advancing pagans. Oliver reproaches his companion for their plight: had he blown his horn, Charles would be here to protect his rearguard; but now it is doomed. Roland's answer is to rail against faint hearts and summon all his comrades to stand sure and strike well. At this, Archbishop Turpin calls the French to him: 'It is our duty to die for our King. Help now to maintain the
Plate 45 Christian faith. But first say your confessions and beg God's mercy; then I shall absolve you all so that if you die, you will be blessed martyrs and have your place in Paradise.' The Franks prostrate themselves before him. He gives his blessing and commands them, as their penance, to strike hard. When they rise again, he signs them with the cross; and then, all finely armed, they mount their battle-steeds.

Plate 47 Count Roland calls to Oliver: 'As you well know, we've been betrayed for gold by Ganelon. The Emperor should avenge us. As for Marsile, he'll have his price with our sword-strokes!' With that he goes brandishing his spear, the gonfalon at its tip white against the sky. With fierce pride he looks at the Saracens, but at the French with mild humility: 'Go gently, noble lords. Today will bring us rich booty, greater than French king has ever won.' When he has spoken these words, the armies clash. But even now Oliver has time for a further reproof for Roland's failure to sound the horn, before himself shouting encouragement to the Franks and calling for
Plate 48 the Emperor's battle-cry. With a great shout of 'Monjoie!' they ride at the infidel.

Marsile's nephew hurls taunts at them: 'Your protector has betrayed you scoundrel Franks. Today France will lose its reputation and the Emperor his own right arm!' This is too much for Roland. He spurs his steed to strike Aelroth with all his might. With his lance he shatters shield, hauberk and spine, casting his foe dead from his horse. 'Charles was right to leave us in the pass. Fair France shall not lose its good name today. Have at them, Franks; this first blow is ours! We're in the right, these villains in the wrong!'

Aelroth's other uncle, Falsaron, whose brow measures a full six inches between the eyes, seeks to avenge his nephew's death and calls out mocking words. But Oliver's blow is no less true than

39 'The King awaits some news of Ganelon
And of the truce with the great land of Spain.
As morning breaks and the clear dawn appears
Count Ganelon arrives back at the camp.'
(ll. 665–8)

On the left stand the Kings of Saragossa, in the centre are the treasure, horses and hostages.

dient quant la matiere le

40 The stage is set for the tragedy, the protagonists stand looking at each other: the venerable Charles with his long beard, his ermine-trimmed sleeves and his sceptre, the elegant Roland, Durendal slung round his slim hips, and, on Roland's left, the crafty-faced Ganelon, presenting an account of his mission. Without, the sumpter horses are being brought to the palace laden with gifts. A subtle touch here is that the cloths covering the bales of goods bear the arms of France and the Empire and one even has Roland's lion. The composition is like a scene from a medieval play: Ganelon is standing on 'stage left', the area which housed the 'Mouth of Hell' on the stage of a mystery play.

41 (Overleaf) Roland proudly leads the rearguard; the Saracens have already planned their ambush: ►

> 'High in the hills they halted in a wood:
> Four hundred thousand wait the break of day.
> Oh God, what grief the French know naught of this!'
>
> (ll. 714–6)

his companion's, and he too jeers at his enemy's corpse before shouting Charlemagne's battle-cry. King Corsablis the Berber then flings his insults at the French, but only to feel the thrust of Archbishop Turpin's lance. As he falls, Turpin mocks him before proclaiming his faith in Charles and crying aloud 'Monjoie!' In the same way Gerin topples Malprimis of Brigant, whose soul is carried off by Satan; Gerier fells the emir, Duke Samson the almanzor, and Anseïs despatches Turgis of Turtelose. Escremis of Valterne is slain by Engelier, the Gascon from Bordeaux, Estorgans by Oton, and Estramariz by Berengier. Of the twelve pagan peers only two remain alive: Margariz and Chernuble. The handsome Margariz spurs at Oliver, shatters his shield with its golden boss, and drives his spear close against the Count's side. But thanks to God's protection Oliver is unscathed. The pagan rides on, sounding his bugle to rally his men.

Plate 49

Plate 61

All now join in the affray. With his lance Roland strikes fifteen blows before its shaft is shattered. Then he draws his sword Durendal and rides at Chernuble. He splits his helmet with its gleaming carbuncles, cuts through the cap beneath, down through the head between the eyes, through the shining hauberk and the whole body's length, through the saddle with its beaten gold, and down through the horse's chine before the force of the blow is spent. 'Mahomet can't help you now!' he calls. And so the Count goes riding about the field, piling corpse on corpse, until his hauberk, both his arms, and even his steed's neck and withers stream with blood.

Nor are Oliver and the twelve peers idle. The shaft of Oliver's lance is broken; but with the stump he knocks a pagan's eyes and brains from his head. Still he smites with it at Saracens, and many fall; but at last the stump is broken right to his fist. Roland sees him: 'Companion, what's that? I don't use sticks in a battle such as this. Where's your sword Halteclere?' Oliver's reply is cutting: 'I couldn't draw it: I was much too busy striking blows'. But then he does unsheathe his sword, shows it to Roland, and at once cleaves a pagan and his horse. 'This is the friend I know!' calls Roland. 'The Emperor loves us for blows like that.' On every hand the cry goes up: 'Monjoie!'

Together Gerin and Gerier topple one infidel to the field, while Engelier of Bordeaux cuts down another. Then the Archbishop slays Siglorel, a sorcerer whom Jupiter through the black arts had once guided down to Hell. And so the battle rages grimly on, with lances shattered, standards torn to shreds, and many fine young Frenchmen ending their days, never to see wives and mothers again, or their comrades who wait with Charlemagne in the pass. The King may lament for them, but his tears are to no avail. No help will come from him. He was ill served that day by Ganelon, says the poet; but the traitor who sold these men in Saragossa was himself to forfeit his life, along with thirty of his kinsmen. (Throughout the Song, as here, there is no attempt to conceal the outcome of events. The aim was not to keep the audience breathless with suspense and surprise, but through the manner of the telling to rouse within them the ache of more profound emotions: grief, pity, awe.)

The peers and their comrades fight on, multiplying the pagan dead. But the French too lose many of their best warriors. In France a frightful tumult fills the air. Tempests blow, rain and hailstones hurtle from the sky, the lightning flashes and the thunder peals, and the entire land quakes. From St. Michael's Mount to Sens and from Besançon to the port of Wissant the walls of every dwelling split. Then at noon a great darkness descends, broken only by the lightning-shafts. All men are seized with terror and cry: 'This is surely the latter end, the Day of Judgement!' But they are wrong; for this is the great agony for Roland's death.

(The first phase of the battle is over, with the Saracens dead on the field or in flight. A moment of muted triumph, one might think; yet this was the time the poet chose to call to our minds the elemental chaos at the time of the Crucifixion and, it may be, the reported wonders that presaged Charlemagne's death. With this we forget for a while Roland's rashness and conceit and see only the ideal epic hero, as if transfigured.)

The French go about the field seeking their kinsmen and mourning the dead. Then with his main army King Marsile appears: twenty Saracen squadrons with shining arms and gilded, gem-studded helmets. Seven thousand bugles sound the charge. Roland calls to Oliver: 'Now Ganelon's treason is plain; but the Emperor will take revenge. In this grim battle I shall strike with Durendal, and you with Halteclere, to such effect that no mocking song shall be sung about them.'

At the head of Marsile's host rides a Saracen, Abisme, an evil infidel, black as melted pitch. When the Archbishop sees him, his only wish is to make an end of such a heretic. So, mounted on his fine mettlesome steed taken from a Danish king he once slew, he spurs to attack the Saracen. The pagan has a gem-studded shield given him by a demon; but it does not have the strength to withstand Turpin's blow. Abisme falls, pierced through the body. 'The Archbishop guards his crozier well!' cry the French.

With the battle joined again, the Christians implore Roland, Oliver, and the peers to give them protection. Turpin senses their fear in the face of such odds and warns them not to flee, though the next day will not see them alive. When he repeats his assurance that the gates of Paradise will stand wide for them, they are filled with gladness, and every man cries out: 'Monjoie!'

Climborin, one of the pagans who took Ganelon's oath and rewarded him in Saragossa, then rides against Engelier and strikes him down. Oliver takes revenge for his comrade on Climborin, whose soul is borne off by devils; and then he slays nine others, prompting Roland's exclamation: 'My companion's annoyed and even vies with me in valour. These are the blows that endear us

42 The suspense mounts: more presages of imminent disaster follow, in Charles's prophetic dreams.

to Charles. Strike on, good knights!' But now the tide is running hard against the Franks, and we see more of the peers fall: Duke Samson, Anseïs, Gerin and Gerier, Berengier. Each combat is described in parallel, almost ritualistic terms: the pagan is characterized, then the swiftness of his horse, the blow he deals, and finally the vengeance wreaked on him by Roland, by Turpin, by Roland again. Yet for all the formalized nature of this grisly dance of death, the poet adds his individual touches: the heathen Valdabrun, who had taken Ganelon's oath, was a great sea-captain who had once seized Jerusalem by guile and slain the Patriarch before the fonts; Grandoine, having just killed three of the peers, recognized Roland by his proud, handsome appearance and tried in vain to flee.

After the series of individual combats, we return to a panoramic view of the battle: the furious blows, the grief and the glory, men wounded and the dead sprawled in heaps, Saracens taking to their heels, bright blood flowing in streams on the green grass, and always Roland, Oliver, and the Archbishop in the thick of it. The poet appeals to records and charters for the tally of the pagan dead: more than four thousand, the annals say. Their first four sallies brought the Franks great success; but from the fifth there came only grief and disaster, for of all the knights from France, only sixty remained alive.

Suddenly, Roland sees the great Christian losses and seems for the first time to become aware of the reality of the situation. He turns to Oliver: 'Comrade, what now? Fair France deserves our pity for the loss of such noble knights. If only the Emperor were here! What can we do? How can we send him this news?' There is more than a touch of bitterness in Oliver's reply: 'I don't know how to tell him. I'd rather die than see us put to shame!'—'I shall blow the oliphant, and Charles will hear it from the pass and turn back to our aid.'—'But that would mean disgrace on your family! You wouldn't do it when I asked, so I'll not advise it now. There would be no courage in that.—But I see both your arms running with gore.'—'I've struck many fine blows,' says Roland. He repeats his proposal, but Oliver will have none of it: had he done it before, they would not be in this plight. 'And, by my beard, if I see my sister Aude again, nevermore will you lie in her arms!'—'Why this bitterness?' asks Roland, uncomprehendingly. 'Companion, the fault is yours. It's better to be prudent than reckless; and it's your temerity that has brought the French to their deaths and lost our service to Charles. We've seen your prowess, Roland, to our cost. You will die here and France be put to shame; and before evening falls, our true comradeship will end.'

(See *Plate 90*)

Why this sudden resolve on Roland's part to sound the ivory horn? Does it show a belated awareness of his sin of pride and rash self-confidence, a movement of repentance and Christian humility? Or is it simply that he feels his duty towards himself and his family honour fully

43 Roland, a youthful figure on his horse, has been appointed captain of the rearguard—and the Franks reluctantly leave him to his fate.

◀ 44 (Opposite) Charles invests Roland with the standard of his command as Turpin and Oliver look on; then the Emperor and the main part of the army sadly wave farewell.

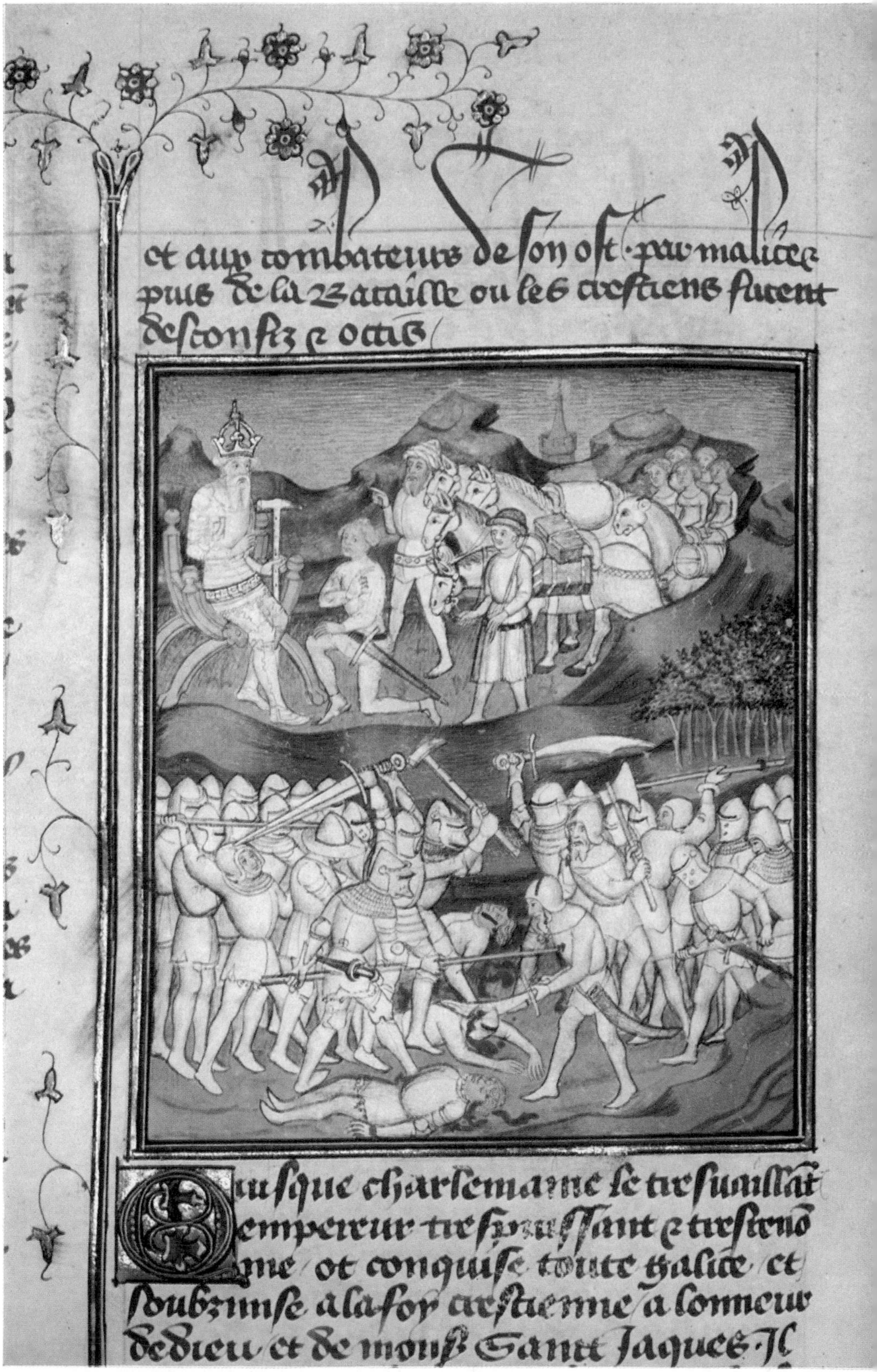

XI Ganelon's return to Charlemagne with the gifts from Saragossa is combined here with the pagan attack on the rearguard.

45 Turpin addresses the Christians before battle:

> ' "Say your confessions, for God's mercy pray!
> I will absolve you to secure your souls.
> If you die, blessed martyrs you will be
> And have your place on high in Paradise."
>
> The French rose up again upon their feet,
> Truly absolved and pardoned for their sins;
> And God's archbishop signed them with the cross.'
>
> (ll. 1132–5; 1139–41)

All the knights then attend Mass served by the archbishop.

pour le mieulx Et conclurent ensemble que
des icelle nuit se partiroient eulx et leurs gens
et se logeroient secretement en lieu dont ilz

46 The Saracen armies mass behind the hills and Roland and Oliver watch their approach from their vantage point. In the foreground the small band of Christians prepare to sell their lives dearly. Roland and Oliver are again shown here, the one with a lion on his shield, the other with a flower.

47 (Overleaf) Ganelon is paid for his services by the Kings of Saragossa. ▶ Above is the first phase of the battle, in which the Franks were victorious.

> 'We have all been betrayed by Ganelon,
> Who has been paid in money, wealth and gold.'
> (ll. 1147–8)

performed and turns his thoughts now to his obligations towards Charles, France, and Christendom? At all events, it was the good Archbishop who brought the quarrel to an end: 'To sound the horn now cannot save us; but still it should be done. The King will come and avenge our deaths on the Spanish infidels. He will put our mangled bodies on biers and have us borne to our burial in hallowed ground.'

Roland sets the oliphant to his lips and gives a blast so powerful that it is heard at thirty *Plates 50–53* leagues. Charles hears it, with all his company. 'Our men are doing battle!' he exclaims. 'From other lips,' says Ganelon, 'this would seem a great lie.' Still Roland blows, and with such force that his mouth runs red with blood, and at his temples his skull has burst. The Emperor says: 'This is Roland's horn, and he never sounded it except in battle.'—'There's no battle,' Ganelon *Plate* XIII retorts. 'Your hair is white with age, yet you speak like a child. You know well enough Roland's great arrogance—I wonder God bears with it so long. He took Noples without your orders: the *Plate 55* Saracens attacked him outside the city, and later he washed the meadows with running streams so you'd not see the blood he'd spilt. He'll blow his horn all day for a mere hare; and now he's *Plate 54* showing off in front of his peers. No one would dare to fight him. Ride on, then! We're still far from our fatherland.' But Naimes shares the King's fear: 'He's doing battle, betrayed by the man who tells you not to act. So arm and shout your battle-cry, then go to aid your men! You can hear Roland is desperate.'

Charlemagne has his own horns sound. The men don their armour and mount, vowing to fight at Roland's side, if they can come in time. But in vain: they have delayed too long. Armour, arms and gonfalons all gleam in the evening sun. The King commands that Ganelon be arrested and *Plate 56* handed over for safe keeping to the royal cooks. A hundred scullions take him, pluck the hair from his beard, drub him with fists and sticks; then they put an iron collar round his neck and chain him like a bear. He is set on a pack-horse's back and kept to be delivered up to Charles when he returns.

Meanwhile, by the deep valleys and shadowy hills the Emperor rides in his wrath, praying for Roland's safety. On the battlefield his nephew sees so many comrades lying dead around him. To *Plate 57* them he addresses a lament, praying that their souls may find Paradise and regretting the end of their long and faithful service to himself, the Emperor, and fair France. 'French lords, you have been slain on my behalf. I cannot be your protector now, but may God give you aid. Oliver, comrade, I must not fail you. If blows do not kill me, I shall die of grief. Let us set to again!' Back into the fray he goes, striking so fiercely that the pagans flee before him like the stag before the hounds. Around him, the remaining Frenchmen fight grimly on.

ma mozt lequel nous a faulsement trahy ·

Comment le noble duc rolant le conte oliuier et les douze pers de france se combatirent a lad
miral marcille qui les faisoit guaittier en la
vallee de ramcheuaulx acompaignes de les gens

48 'Pagans and Saracens, see them now come to grips!' (l.1187) The ranks of turbaned Saracens stretch to the horizon; against them Roland and the peers make a brave charge.

49 The prowess of Turpin and Roland. The engagements follow the traditional pattern of combat with lances, then with swords.

Plate 58 Now Marsile himself approaches on his steed Gaignon. Bevon, lord of Beaune and Dijon,
falls at his attack; and then he slays the peers Yvon, Yvoire, and Gerard of Roussillon. Seeing
Plate XII this, Roland makes for him with Durendal, strikes off his right hand, and then turns to lop the
head from his son Jurfaleu the Fair. The infidels call upon their gods, then a hundred thousand
turn in flight, and Marsile with them. But his uncle Marganice is still on the field with his hideous
black troops from Ethiopia, who have nothing white about them but their teeth. Once again
Plate XIV Roland rallies his men to the attack; but the pagans are bolder now, seeing the mere handful
of surviving French. Marganice sets his golden spurs into his horse and strikes at Oliver's back.
He forces home the spear so that it comes out through his breast: 'Your loss alone is enough to
avenge all of ours!' Though Oliver feels his death-blow has been struck, with a curse on his foe
he brings his sword down through his golden, jewelled helmet and his skull. Then he calls Roland
to his aid before turning back into the press and, with a shout of 'Monjoie!', sending more Saracens to their doom.

'Roland, companion, come and stand at my side!' he calls. 'This day will see us part in bitter
Plate 59 grief.' Roland sees how his face has lost all colour, while from his wound the blood pours to
the ground. With words of pity for his friend, for France, and for Charles, he himself swoons
as he sits in the saddle. Oliver has lost so much blood that his sight has gone; and when Roland
approaches him, he strikes him with his sword, cleaving his helmet in two, but leaving his head
untouched. The blow brings Roland to his senses; and looking at his companion, he asks him in
a gentle voice if he has struck him on purpose. Oliver says: 'Now I hear you speak, but cannot see
you; may God keep you in His sight. I struck you? Forgive me then, I beg you.' Roland replies:
'I've come to no harm. You have my pardon here in the sight of God.' Each bows towards the
other's breast. 'See,' says the poet, 'with what love they to their parting come!'

Plate 60 Oliver feels that death presses him hard. Leaving his horse, he prostrates himself on the ground and with clasped hands makes his confession, asking God's blessing on France and Charles, and most of all on his companion Roland. His helmet falls forward, and his heart beats no more. Never was there grieving greater than Roland's at his death. Softly he laments him: 'Together we've seen so many years pass; and never have you harmed me or I wronged you. Now you are dead, my life is but pain.' With that he swoons upon his horse, with only his gold stirrups holding him secure.

Down from the mountains comes Gautier de l'Hum. All his men have been slaughtered there by the pagans, and he himself is sorely wounded. His call for aid brings Roland from his swoon. Of the Franks only these two and the Archbishop now remain, and together they send a score or

50 'The oliphant is set to Roland's lips;
He holds it firm and sounds it with great power.
High are the hills, and the call carries far.'
(ll. 1753–5)

51 'Charles heard it sound and all his company.
"Our men are doing battle", said the King.
And Ganelon flung back these words at him:
"From other lips great falsehood this would seem!" '

(ll. 1757–60)

lusen mort. den dir marsilie gap. ich gerich iz
b ich mac. war bedorfestu des. dar zu spranc

52 'Count Roland spares no effort and no pains;
With agony he sounds his oliphant.'
(ll. 1761–2)

saint Jaques et plusieurs autres Et quant il eut chasse les
sarrazins hors du regne Il se mist au retour vers france
La bataille de raincheuaulx et la mort rolant et olivier

XII Resplendent in the blue and gold of France, Durendal at the ready, Roland confronts a pagan over the dead and dying on the battlefield. In the far distance, Roland blows his horn and the sun glints on the helmets of the heathen army.

more pagans to their deaths. Round them a thousand Saracens gather, fearing to approach. Instead they hurl lances, spears, darts and arrows from a distance. Gautier is slain at their first volley, and Turpin suffers great wounds in head and body, while his steed is killed beneath him. 'I'm not vanquished yet!' cries the Archbishop and hews about him with his sword. Charles was to tell afterwards that he found four hundred of the infidels around him dead or dying; so say the annals penned by St. Giles in Laon's great church.

Roland fights on, his body bathed in sweat, and a great aching in his head where his temples are burst. But again he blows the horn, feebly now; and Charles, who hears it, knows his end is near. He orders his men to ride faster still, and calls for all the bugles to be blown. Sixty thousand ring out; and hearing the clamour, the pagans realize that the Emperor is near and that, should he find his nephew alive, he will renew the Spanish war to their great loss. Once more they press a savage attack on Roland, who takes his stand beside the unhorsed Turpin. And still they cannot vanquish him: instead they hurl their javelins and shafts, striking down Veillantif beneath him and shattering his shield and mail, but without making a single wound on his body. Then they turn tail, full of wrath and grief.

Plate 62

With his steed dead, Roland cannot pursue the fugitives. He goes instead to Turpin, tenderly strips him of his armour, and cuts his tunic into pieces to bind his great wounds. Embracing him then and gently laying him on the grass, he asks his leave to go and seek out the dead peers. Begging him to return soon, the Archbishop exclaims: 'Thanks be to God, this field is yours and mine.' So Roland scours the hills and vales. There he finds Gerin and Gerier, Berengier, Oton, Samson, Anseïs, and old Gerard of Roussillon; and one by one he bears them to place them in a row at Turpin's knees. The man of God gives his benison, saying he too will die in grief never to see the Emperor again. Last of all, Roland brings his companion Oliver and for him makes a final grief-stricken lament. All colour drains from his face, and he falls fainting to the ground.

When Turpin sees the Count swoon, he takes his oliphant and falteringly makes towards a stream that flows through Roncevaux to fetch him water, if he can. But he has lost so much blood that soon he topples on his face. Roland recovers his senses and sees him lying on the grass, praying with joined hands that God grant him Paradise. Then death takes Turpin, Charles's great warrior and true champion against the infidel in sermon and in fight. There he lies, his brains and entrails spilling on the ground, and his delicate white hands crossed upon his breast. For him too Roland speaks a sorrowful lament, commending his soul to God.

Then the Count feels his own death drawing near. Thinking even now of his reputation, he takes the oliphant and Durendal his sword, and goes towards Spain to climb a hillock where four marble blocks stand beneath a tree. There his strength fails him yet again; and as he lies swooning, a Saracen, who has smeared himself with blood and lies feigning death, leaps up thinking to take the hero's sword back as a trophy to Arabia. But as he tugs at it, Roland comes to. He raises the oliphant and with it strikes him on his helm, shattering his skull and bursting his eyes from their sockets. 'You were too bold, foul heathen, to lay hands on me. But now my oliphant is split at its mouth, and the crystal and gold have fallen away.'

Plate 63

Plate 64, XV

The Count struggles to his feet to try and break Durendal on a dark stone that stands there. Ten times he strikes, hacking away much of the stone; but the sword rebounds towards the sky, the steel grating loud but showing not so much as a notch. As he strikes, Roland addresses it: 'Alas, good Durendal, so long you have been wielded by a fine vassal; but now with my death you will be left without a master. Once Charles was in the vales of Maurienne when God sent an angel to bid him give you to a captain count; and the noble king girt you on me. With you I conquered for him Anjou, Brittany, Poitou and Maine, Normandy, Provence, Aquitaine as well as the Romagna, Lombardy, Flanders and Bavaria, Burgundy and all Apulia. Constantinople too I won for him, and Saxony, Scotland and Ireland, and England that he now holds in his sway. I'd die to save you from the infidel! Your gilded hilt is full of relics: St. Peter's tooth, St. Basil's blood, hairs from the head of St. Denis, part of the blessed Mary's garment. You should serve Christian men alone.'

Feeling death's grip closing, he runs to prostrate himself beneath a pine. Lying there on the green grass, he places beneath him oliphant and sword, then sets his face towards pagan Spain so that Charles and his company will say: 'This noble Count had died a conqueror.' Beating his breast time and again, he makes his confession, remembering all his sins, great and small; and with his thoughts turning to his many conquests, to fair France and his kinsmen, to Charlemagne his lord, and to his own need for divine mercy and protection, he offers up his right glove to God. The blessed Gabriel receives it from his hand and then, with St. Michael and the angel Cherubim, bears his soul up to Paradise.

Plate XVI

Charles and his army come to Roncevaux and find the whole field covered with Christian and pagan dead. Calling aloud for his nephew and the twelve peers, the Emperor tears his beard and gives vent to his grief, while tears fill the eyes of all his knights, and twenty thousand fall in a swoon. Then, with the men mourning their lost kinsmen, friends, and lords, Naimes shows his true gallantry by addressing the first words to Charlemagne: 'Look over there, two leagues ahead: see how the dust-clouds rise! The pagans are there in strength. Ride on, and avenge our grief!'—'Oh God', says Charles, 'they are so far away! But may honour and justice be done, for they have

Comment le duc rolant ſonna ſon olifant contre
la voulente de oliuier ſon compaignon lequel
len auoit par auant requis tant inſtamment

53 'Count Roland's mouth runs red with his own blood,
And at the temple he has burst his skull.
He sounds the oliphant with toil and pain.'
(ll. 1785–7)

robbed me of the flower of France.' He commands four lords to guard the whole field and ensure that the dead are untouched by man or beast. Then he has his bugles sound and with his great host rides on in pursuit of the infidels.

But when he sees that the evening is falling, he dismounts to lie on the ground and pray to God that He make the sun stand still and the night delay. In answer to his prayer an angel, with whom he often spoke, appears to him with the assurance that vengeance will be his. God works a mighty miracle for Charlemagne, staying the sun in the heavens. The Franks drive on, catch up with the Saracens as they flee through the Val Tenebros and, slaying them as they go, force them towards the deep, swift waters of the Ebro before Saragossa. Finding no boats, the surviving pagans leap into the river. But there is no escape: those who are heavily armoured sink in its depths, the rest are swept away. The Frenchmen cry: 'Alas, Roland, for you!'

With all the pagans dead, Charlemagne falls to the ground to give thanks to God; and when he rises again, the sun has set. It is too late then to return to Roncevaux, so there in open country he sets up his camp, while the horses are turned to graze in the meadows. That night no sentinel is set. But the Emperor will not take off his armour or unlace his gilded, jewelled helmet. At his side as he lies the splendid Joyeuse is girt, his sword that changes colour thirty times a day and in whose gilded pommel is set the tip of the lance with which Christ was wounded on the cross. From its name, says the poet, the French took their battle-cry, 'Monjoie!' So Charles lies at rest, grieving for Roland, Oliver, and the peers. But his anguish has so wearied him that at length he falls asleep. Throughout the meadows the Franks sleep too; and even the horses are so exhausted that if they wish to graze, they must do so lying down. 'He has learned much who has known suffering', the poet says.

(At this point there begins the first of the controversial sections of the Song which introduce the figure of the Emir Baligant. Their content can be given more briefly, partly because they know Roland only as a memory, but partly because there is less economy in the verse itself, and the whole speed of narration slackens. At the same time, Charlemagne becomes a more energetic and dominant figure, while the spirit of militant Christianity gains in prominence. It is as if the breath of the First Crusade has passed over the episode with its final, apocalyptic clash.)

Charles, then, sleeps like a tormented man; but all night he is guarded by Gabriel, who reveals through a vision a great battle that he must soon face. From a storm-racked sky fire descends to kindle the shafts and shields of his company, who are assaulted by all manner of beasts and demons. They cry for the Emperor's help; but he is attacked by a lion and cannot come, nor can he tell which of them will win the struggle.

54 Many times Roland had routed the heathen with the mere sound of his oliphant and once he captured a city with its aid. Yet Ganelon attempts to dismiss the call for help.

onques sarrazin ne lauoit ainsi abuse.
Coment le roy fourze fu occis contre le gre de lēpereur par oliuier de vienne qui vengia la mort de son frere gerier que fourre auoit occis Et-

55 Ganelon addresses Charlemagne:

' "Full well you know Roland's great arrogance;
I marvel that God bears with it so much!
Noples he took without your bidding it:
Out from the city burst the Saracens,
And Roland the good vassal they attacked;
Later with running streams he washed the fields
So that you should not see the blood he'd spilt." '
(ll. 1773–9)

56 Convinced of his treachery,

'The King commands Count Ganelon's arrest
And has him handed to the royal cooks.'
(ll. 1816–7)

cognoissance comme de la bataille et du juge-
ment sera cy apres faitte mention au long.
Si se taist a tant listoire de la piteuse desco-
fiture de ramcheuaulx et deuise

si uon dem wal. rechte sam di hunte. si riefen
alle mit munde. hilf uns chunic marsilie. herre.
durch dine chunecliche ere. di cristen sint starc

57 Meanwhile in the pass of Roncevaux, the rearguard is hard-pressed. Roland spurs Veillantif across the field in pursuit of the heathen.

King Marsile has fled to Saragossa and, disarming, lies on the grass there faint from the loss of blood from his maimed right arm. Queen Bramimonde grieves for him, then runs to beat and shatter their faithless gods Apollyon, Tervagant, and Mahomet. The king is borne to a vaulted room, where Bramimonde continues her lament and declares the Emir a coward if he will not do battle with the French and their white-bearded Emperor.

In the first year of Charles's Spanish campaign Marsile had sent letters to summon from Cairo Baligant, the aged Emir who had outlived both Homer and Virgil. Though Baligant had delayed long, he had summoned his men from forty kingdoms and had a great fleet fitted out in a port by Alexandria. On the first day of summer he committed his ships to the sea. At night so many were the lanterns and carbuncles shining from masts and prows that the whole sea was lit up, and the land too when they approached the Spanish coast. They sailed up the Ebro, and at Saragossa Baligant and his mighty retinue disembarked. Seated on an ivory throne, the Emir held council, vowing to carry his challenge to Charlemagne as far as Aix, if need be. Two messengers, Clarifan and Clarïen, were to take this news to Marsile and bid him pay homage for his fief.

The messengers ride through Saragossa and up to the palace, where all is grief and bitterness. Their greeting in the name of the pagan trinity meets with a woeful denunciation of these gods by Queen Bramimonde; but when they speak of Baligant's determination to pursue the Emperor to France, she tells them there is no need to go so far, for the Franks are close at hand. The mortally wounded Marsile says that if the Emir will come to him, he will surrender his Spanish fief for Baligant to defend henceforth. He hands the messengers the keys of Saragossa, and they depart.

They bear the news of the pagan defeat and Marsile's plight to Baligant, and tell of Charles's presence on the Ebro's banks. The Emir's eyes flash with pride, and joy fills his heart. To his lords he gives the order to mount and ride; and with four of his leaders he himself sets forth for Saragossa. In the palace he is met by Bramimonde and taken to the chamber where the King lies. The stricken Marsile hands Baligant a glove in token of his surrender of his lands. Then the Emir spurs back to his main company and, riding ahead of them, urges them on against the Christians.

The scene now reverts to Charlemagne and, perhaps, to the more primitive substance of the Song. We see the Emperor waking from his dream-filled sleep, being signed with the cross by the angel Gabriel, and along with the rest of his men putting off his armour. Then they gallop together back to Roncevaux. Coming upon the field, Charles goes ahead, remembering that Roland had once boasted he would never die on foreign soil save at the head of all his troops and peers. And there on the hill, amid the bloodstained flowers, the Emperor sees the mark of Roland's

Ci parle du messagr ganelon Et de
la traison quil fist aux francois et aux
bons chlrs de france Et des presens que les
sarrazins firent au Roy Charlem et aux
combatemens par malice Et puis de la ba
taille coment le crestiens furet occis

58 Roland, with a coronet round his helm, charges down on Marsile, his arm raised for the blow which will cut off his adversary's hand. Marsile faces him, a plume floating from his helmet. All the violence and confusion of medieval combat is conveyed in this packed scene.

sword on the stone, and his nephew's body lying on the grass. Charles runs to embrace him, swoons upon his body, and is caught up by Naimes, Geoffrey of Anjou, Thierry his brother, and Count Acelin. He begins his lament, but again faints away before rousing himself and putting his great grief into words: 'Friend Roland, may God raise your soul to bliss. How wrong I was to bring you into Spain! Who now will there be to maintain my honour? Each day I shall weep for you, and all my strength and ardour will decline. When I come to France and my own court at Laon, men will arrive from many lands asking for you; and I shall say that you are dead in Spain. To Aix they will come asking for news; and I shall give the grim news that my nephew, victor in my wars, is dead. Then the Saxons will rise against me, Bulgars, Hungarians, foes from Italy and Africa. But whom shall I find to lead my armies? Such is my grief that I would live no longer! God grant that before I reach the main pass of Cize my soul may quit my body to find its abode with my slain company; and let my flesh be buried beside theirs!'

Plates 66–68, XVI

At this, Geoffrey of Anjou seeks to comfort him, suggesting that the slain Christians be gathered for burial in a single grave. 'Sound your horn,' says Charles, 'it shall be done!' And so it is that the slain are buried together with much honour, absolved and blessed by bishops, abbots, and other men of God amid the fragrance of incense and myrrh. Charles has the bodies of Roland, Oliver, and the Archbishop opened before his eyes. Their hearts are wrapped in a silken cloth and placed in a white marble coffin, while their bodies, washed in perfumes and wine, are wrapped in stag-hides to be carried in three carts beneath cloths of Eastern silk.

Plates 69, 70

Suddenly we are back with Baligant, whose challenge is borne to Charles by two messengers. The Emperor calls his barons to arms, himself mounting his steed Tencendur, with Joyeuse girt at his side. Two lords, Rabel and Guinemant, are bidden to take sword and oliphant and fill the posts of Roland and Oliver. There follows an account of the drawing up of the ten Christian divisions, formed of men from all parts of France as well as Bavarians, Germans, Flemings and Frisians. In the tenth are the great Frankish barons, a hundred thousand grey-haired, white-bearded lords. With them rides the Emperor, and Geoffrey of Anjou bears his royal standard, the oriflamme. With a shout of 'Monjoie!' the knights call for action. But first Charles falls to the earth to pray for God's protection so that he may avenge Roland's death.

Plates 71, 72

The Emperor mounts again and rides proudly forth. To front and rear the bugles resound, the oliphant ringing above the rest. For pity of Roland all the Frenchmen weep. So Charles rides on, his beard lying on his byrnie's breast like those of his men, who wear them thus for love of him. On they ride to the Spanish march, where they take their stand in a plain. Meanwhile, the messengers have returned to Baligant; and he too calls his men to arms.

The Saracen drums beat out, their trumpets and bugles sound. The pagans don their armour, Baligant girding on his sword Precieuse, so called to vie with that of Charles, its name used also as his battle-cry. Baligant cuts a splendid figure with his broad chest, narrow hips, proud open countenance, and curly hair: 'God, what a lord, were he a Christian!' His son Malpramis is a fine knight too and eager for the advance; but he doubts if Charles will wait to fight. Baligant knows better, saying he has had a report of the Emperor's return, but is confident that, without Roland, the Christians cannot withstand the pagan might. Malpramis craves the first blow in the battle, and this the Emir grants, with a great fief, though his son will not enter into its possession.

Baligant then draws up his own thirty divisions, formed from as many strange races. Some of his men have huge heads, and bristled spines along their backs; others have hides as hard as iron and fight without helmets or hauberks. But hideous or not, all ride valiantly. The Emir has his dragon standard borne ahead, while ten Canaanites ride among his troops, calling upon the pagans to worship and serve their gods with humility. Then Baligant sends forward his son with the kings Torleu and Dapamort and all but his own three divisions to join in battle with Charlemagne. The two armies sight each other in open country. Once more the Christian bugles peal forth, and the oliphant louder than them all.

To his brother Canabeu Baligant points out the Emperor and his company, their beards shining on their byrnies as white as snow on ice. Then he rides to the front of all his troops and, brandishing his great spear, calls: 'Come pagans, I start on my way!' When Charlemagne sees him, he too calls on his men to join him in battle with the Saracens. He sets his spurs into his horse; and Tencendur makes four great leaps for him. With that, the first divisions lock in combat.

The fighting starts with Count Rabel thrusting his lance through Torleu the Persian king, then Guinemant attacks and slays a king of Lycia. But the Emir's son Malpramis hurls himself among the Franks and wreaks great slaughter, with Baligant calling the infidels to lend him support. In this fearsome battle there will be no truce. Time and again the Emir urges his men on, promising to reward them well with fiefs and beautiful women. Charlemagne too cries that he will repay his barons with wealth and lands, but most of all he exhorts them to avenge their kinsfolk slain in Roncevaux. He will never be deserted by his Franks.

Seeing the havoc wrought by Malpramis, Duke Naimes makes for him and, with a great lance-thrust, casts him dead amid seven hundred others. At once King Canabeu spurs after Naimes, bringing his sword down on the Duke's helmet and leaving him wounded and stunned. But Charlemagne himself is prompt to avenge the stroke; and with the pagan dead, he and the wounded Naimes ride side by side. The Emir, meanwhile, does not spare his blows, but with his infidels

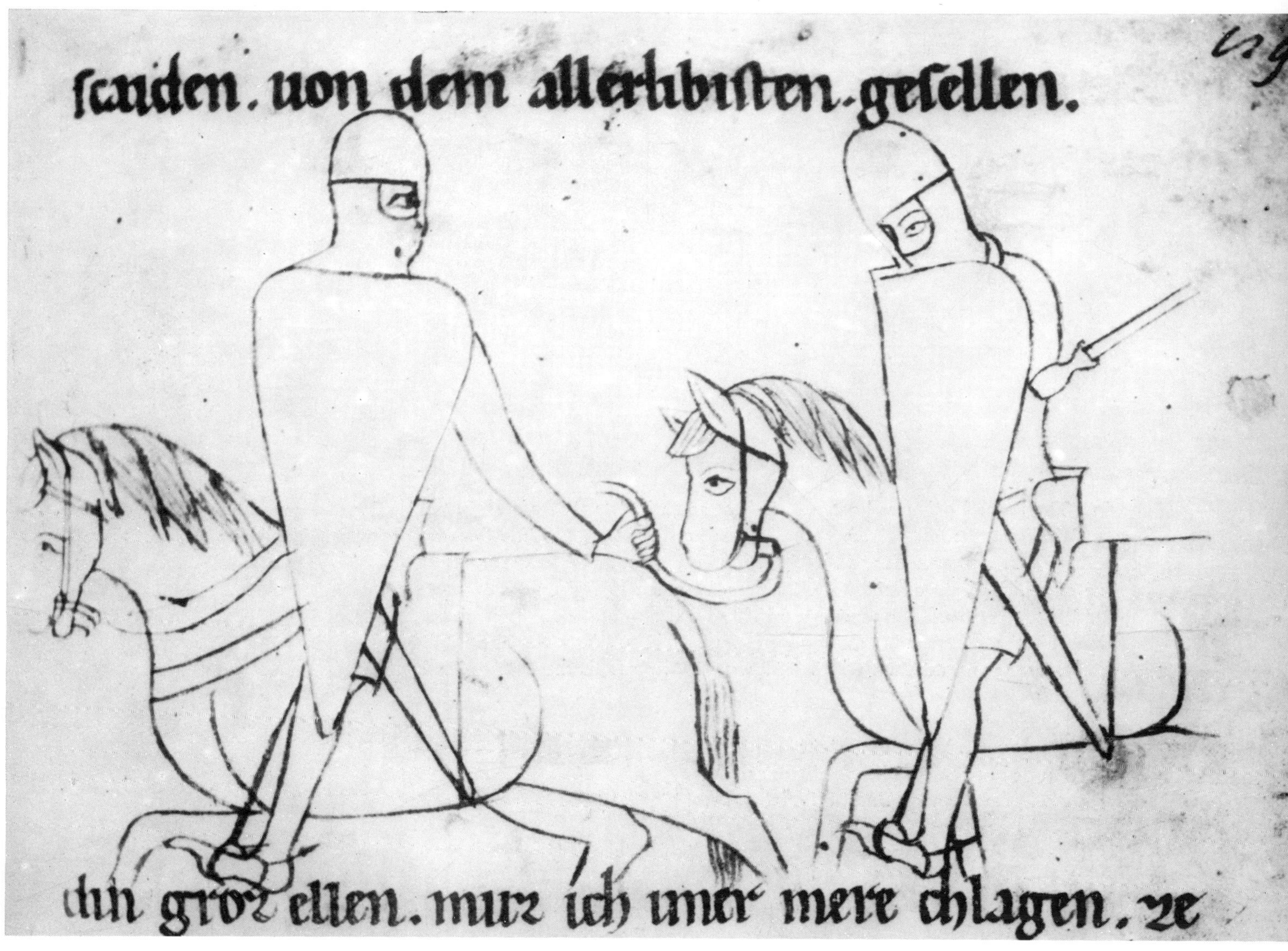

ſcaiden. uon dem allerlibiſten. geſellen.
din groz ellen. muz ich imer mere chlagen. ze

59 Roland comes up to his wounded companion-in-arms and

> '. . . sees how the face of Oliver
> Is ashen, livid, colourless and wan.'
> (ll. 1978–9)

Tenderly he leads his horse from the field.

60 The Roland epic was known in Italy at an early date. It featured in the border of a mosaic pavement laid in Brindisi cathedral in 1178 for Archbishop William, a Frenchman. Unfortunately this was entirely destroyed in an earthquake in 1858, and the only records now extant are early nineteenth-century copies, one of which is reproduced here. Reading from left to right, we see Turpin mediating in the quarrel between Roland and Oliver, who is not shown in Schultz's copy, then Roland bearing the body of a knight to lay alongside the five already on the ground for Turpin to bless. The blessing is suggested by the angel descending from Heaven and the stalk with five flowers growing from the heads of the knights, reminiscent of Roland's words:

' "...may God His mercy show
And grant His Paradise to all your souls
And give them rest amid celestial flowers!" ' (ll. 1854–6)

In the next scene, Oliver lies dead, clasping his battle-axe. His soul leaves his body in the form of a naked child. Roland leans weeping on his sword. Behind is a 'flash-back' to Roland leading Oliver from the battle on his horse. A final scene, not shown here, depicts Roland slaying the pagan who tried to steal Durendal.

61 As skirmish follows skirmish in the parallel *laisses* of the poem, so scenes of battling knights succeed one another in the *Ruolantes Liet* of Conrad the Priest. Here Engelier of Gascony is shown charging at the head of his company, sword at the ready.

gegen der herte. da frumt er mit dem swer
te. manigen hauden toten. manigen helm
uerscroten. manige tiefe wunden. got behilt
in wol gesunden. daz im an deme libe nine
war. im geuiel uz der scar. achzer unt hun

62 The heathen close in on Turpin and Roland, who now blows a last blast on his horn. The dying Turpin is embraced by Roland, who then smites down the pagan who tries to rob him of Durendal, a mighty blow which cracks the oliphant.

XIII Charlemagne hears Roland's horn and raises his hand to his breast in alarm. At his side, Ganelon attempts to make light of the sound.

63–64 Roland is dying. He kills the thieving Saracen, tries to break Durendal and is found by Thierry.

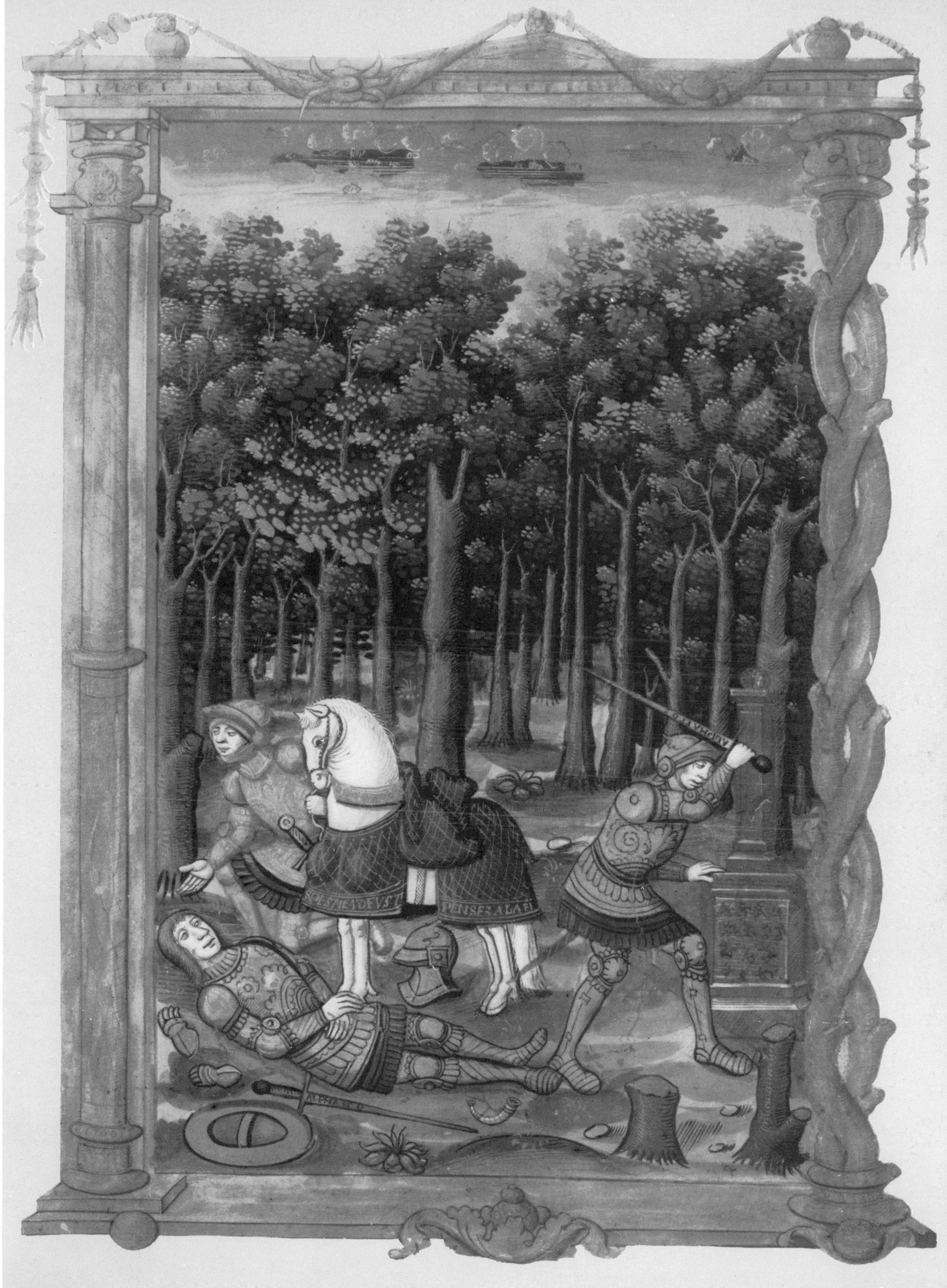

Puis que · kl'm · li
tres puissans ē
preuues et tres re
nōme ot conquise
toute galice · et
soumise a la foi
crestienne lonneur de dieu
et de monseigneur · s · iaq̄
il retourna en france et fist
ses ols herbergier · delez pā
pelune · En ce temps demo
rerent en la cite de sarra

receussent baptesme · Ou
que il li enuoiassent treu ·
Et il li enuoierent pour lui
deceuoir · xx · cheuaux dor
chargies et dargent · et
dautres richesces · Et autres
· xl · chargies de tres pur vin
et tres dous · qui presente
rent aus princes et aus
combateeurs de lost · Et
· cc · belles sarrazines pour
euls seruir en pechie de

◂ XIV Roland, in the fleurs-de-lys of France, meets the Saracen onslaught.

65 The stricken Marsile flees back to Saragossa to die and his Queen Bramimonde has the false gods destroyed.

66–67 Charlemagne mourns Roland on the battlefield. The miniature on the right also shows the flayed body of Oliver and, at the top, the execution of Ganelon in front of Charlemagne and his court.

68–69 Charlemagne looks down from his horse on the body of Roland as he lies with Durendal and the oliphant at his side.

> ‘ “God,” said the King, “how dire is my dismay
> Not to have been here to begin the fray!”
> He plucks his beard like a man racked with grief;
> Tears fill the eyes of all his baron knights.’
>
> (ll. 2412–5)

The heroes’ bodies are wrapped in deer-hides and carried in a litter to Blaye.

gna ⁊ emporta lonneur soustenant lac
cusement vray quil auoit fait. Lors le
Roy commanda prendre gannes ꝑ les
quatre membres ⁊ atacher a quatre che
uaulx tirans chascun dune part qui le
desmēbrerent ⁊ ainsi fina miserablemēt
ses iours.

Adoncques estoient deux cymi
tieres principaulx Cest assauoir
lung a arelate/lautre a burdegalle les
quelz nostre seigneur auoit consacrez
par les mains de sept saincts antistes
cest assauoir de maximin euesque de ac
quense de trop fin a telatence/de pol de
nerbōne/de saturnin de thoulouze/ De
fronton de pierregort/de marcial de ly
moges ⁊ de eutrope de sainctes/en ces
deux cymitieres fut enseuelie la plus
grant ꝑtie des mors/mais le roy char
lemaigne fist emporter Rolland sur .ii
mulletz en vne litiere doree couuerte
de poelles de drap dor ⁊ de saye iusques
a blaye ⁊ en leglise de mōseigneur sāct
rōmain/laq̃lle il auoit fait faire ⁊ fon
der chanoines reiglez le fist enseuelir/⁊
puis en lonneur de iesucrist fist pendre

De la sepulture des
cheualiers tuez a ron
ceuaulx. XXI.

70 The bodies of Roland and Oliver borne on litters. Oliver's arms, the maiden's head, are clearly distinguishable. Charles raises his clenched hands above his head in an eloquent gesture of grief, and his knights raise their hands to their eyes.

> 'The King commands Tebald and Geboin,
> Milon the Count and the Marquis Oton:
> "Escort them on the highway in three carts." '
>
> (ll. 2970–2)

sends many Christians to their doom. Everywhere shafts and shields are shattered, and the ringing of hauberks mingles with the grating of shield on helmet; and what grief it is to see knights falling, and screaming men dying where they lie.

A pagan reports to the Emir the slaying of his son and his uncle, one of them, he thinks, cut down by the Emperor. Baligant calls the wise Jangleu to tell him how he thinks the battle will end. Jangleu's advice is grim indeed: 'You are dead, Baligant! Your gods will never protect you now against Charles and the Franks. But call up the lords of Occiant, the Arabs, Giants, Enfruns and Turks. Whatever the outcome, don't delay!' Some of these infidels bray and neigh, others bark and yelp like dogs; but they attack the Franks so dashingly that they leave seven thousand dead. The Christian lords, seeing their divisions break, renew their own assault with zest. Ogier the Dane brings down the pagan standard-bearer; and when Baligant sees the royal ensign fall, he begins to realize that right is on the side of Charlemagne.

In the thick of the battle, the Emir shouts his war-cry 'Precieuse!' and Charles 'Monjoie!' *Plate* XVII
Each recognizes the other by his loud, clear voice; and at once they charge together to deal and take great blows. Their horses' girths burst with the shock, the saddles slip, and both men fall to the ground. They draw their swords and fight on, hacking their shields to pieces and from their helmets striking fiery sparks. This is a combat that will never cease unless one of them admits he is in the wrong.

Baligant urges Charles to repent and become his vassal, whereupon the Emperor calls to his adversary to espouse the Christian faith. 'Your homily starts ill,' replies Baligant; and the struggle is resumed. But now the Emir deals Charles such a blow that his helmet is split and his skull laid bare where the sword has sliced through the hair. Charles staggers and almost falls. But this is not God's will; so the angel Gabriel returns to him and asks: 'What are you doing, mighty king?' When Charles hears the angel's voice, his wits and his strength return. With the sword of France he strikes the Emir with such force that his whole head is split down to the beard. 'Monjoie!' he calls to rally his men. Duke Naimes comes up with Tencendur, and the Emperor remounts.

At Baligant's death the pagans flee, with Charles and the Franks hot in pursuit. The King calls to his men: 'Now avenge your grief and work out all your wrath!' Few of the pagans make their escape. The dust-clouds rises in the sun's heat as the chase is carried right to Saragossa. There Queen Bramimonde climbs her tower with all her priests of the false faith, crying
to Mahomet for aid and bringing to Marsile the news of the Emir's end. When he hears, Marsile *Plate* 73
turns to the wall, his face tearful and downcast. Straightway he dies of grief and yields up his soul to the fiends of Hell.

Plate 74 It remains to Charlemagne to take the city, made over to him by the Queen. That night a thousand Franks comb Saragossa, smashing the idols in mosques and synagogues, and leaving no trace of the false faith. The bishops bless the waters in the baptistries, where over a hundred thousand pagans are made Christian. Those who refuse are hanged or burnt, except for Bramimonde: she is to be taken to France, for the King wishes that she should take the faith through love. The Baligant episode has ended on a note of triumph.

When the day dawns, Charlemagne mounts with all his men, except for a thousand knights *Plates* 75, 76, XVIII left to garrison the captured city; and joyfully they take the road back into France. On their way they storm Narbonne; and on St. Seurin's altar in Bordeaux Charles leaves the oliphant filled with gold coins, where it may still be seen by pilgrims. At Blaye, in the church of St. Romain, Roland, Oliver, and the Archbishop are laid to rest in white coffins. At last the Emperor is back in his palace in Aix; and from there he summons his judges for the trial of Ganelon: Saxons, Bavarians, Germans, Frisians, Normans and Bretons, men from Burgundy, Lorraine, and Poitou, along with the wisest men of France.

When Charlemagne has entered his palace, the fair damsel Aude comes before him, asking for news of Roland, who was to take her as his bride. Tears fill the Emperor's eyes, and he plucks at his beard: 'My dear, . . . sweet friend, it is of a dead man you ask.—But I will give you very fair exchange. I mean Louis, my son and heir'.—'These are strange words,' Aude replies. *Plate* XIX 'With Roland dead, please God I may not live on!' All her colour drains, and she falls lifeless at Charles's feet. He thinks she has only swooned away, and takes her to raise her up; but her head droops on her shoulder, and the King sees she is truly dead. He has her carried to a convent, watched by four countesses through the night, then buried with great honour beside an altar.

Outside the palace Ganelon is bound to a stake to await his trial and is well beaten with sticks and staves. One day of high festival, St. Sylvester's Day as some tell, the royal vassals *Plate* 77 assemble in Charles's chapel, and the trial begins. Ganelon is dragged before the Emperor, who calls for judgement: 'He came with me in my army to Spain, and for gain he betrayed my nephew, with Oliver and the twelve peers, and twenty thousand of my Franks.' Ganelon replies: 'Roland once cheated me in goods and gold. That's why I sought to destroy him, but there's no treason in that.' The French deliberate. 'Now hear me, lords,' says Ganelon, 'for the love of God! In the Emperor's army I served him loyally. But in his hatred, Roland tried to send me to my death. I took the message to Marsile, and came safely back by my own wits. But I had defied Roland, Oliver, and all their comrades openly, before Charles and his noble barons. I have taken revenge, but have not betrayed.' The Franks say they will take counsel.

XV 'Roland ſtrikes hard upon a swarthy ſtone,
Cuts more of it away than I could tell.
Loud grates the sword, but does not break or snap.'
(ll. 2338–40)

71 The army of Baligant arrives to fight Charles. Below, the two rulers are unhorsed.

XVI ' "Roland, dear friend, may God His mercy show
And in His Paradise receive your soul." '
(ll. 2933–4)

enclos et qui ne peurent fuir demourerent
illec et furent occis et mis en piteux point.
Comment la cite de sarragoce fu conquise et
comment le roy marcille moru de couroux.

72 Marsile lies dying in Saragossa as the Christians storm the gates.

ne demy ains mort de dueil ainsi que cy apres
sera dit Et atant sen taist listoire et deuise.
Comment baligant fu desconfy et mort en ba
taille par charlemaine et conquis sarragoce.
Istoire dist que quant mazalle et

73 A messenger from Baligant's army brings his challenge to Charlemagne.

daz wert ouch wol die lenge.
daz mir von anegenge.
Gemachet vn̄ geheizen ist.
daz mir der heilige crist.
mit sinem blůte gekoufet hat.
wilt du haben minen rat.
So geloube an den mitalle.
der uns von adames valle.
mit siner marter hat erkouft.
wirdestu durch in getouft.
und behaltest sin gebot.
vn̄ verkiusest din apgot.
er git mer rihtůmes.
und eren vn̄ růmes.
denne alles menschen kunne
uf der erden ie gewunne

74 The defeated Queen Bramimonde surrenders Saragossa to Charles.

◄ XVII 'Now with great vigour they have drawn their swords.
Never will this combat of theirs be stopped:
Only with one man dead its end will come.'

When Charles is prompted by an angel,

'He strikes the Emir with the sword of France,
Shatters his helmet where the gems blaze forth,
Cleaves his head open and spills out the brains.'
(ll. 3576–8; 3615–7)

XVIII The funeral of the dead of Roncevaux in the Church of St. Romain at Blaye.

Thirty of Ganelon's kinsfolk are there, led by the valiant Pinabel of the Château de Sorence. When Ganelon asks his aid, he replies: 'If any Frenchman calls for your death and matches us in combat, then with my sword I'll prove him in the wrong!' The vassals discuss their verdict, the thought of Pinabel making them choose their words; and all but Thierry, the brother of Geoffrey of Anjou, agree to ask for Ganelon's acquittal, on condition that in future he serve Charles loyally. Roland cannot be restored, and only a fool would want to duel now. When the king hears their judgement, he cries: 'You all play me false!' His head sinks on his breast, so grieved he is.

Now Thierry steps before him, a man of middle size, lean, swarthy, and black-haired: 'Forget your distress, lord. You know how faithfully I have served you, and that my high birth gives me the right to put this case: though Roland may have cheated Ganelon, he should have been safe in your service; betraying that is Ganelon's real crime, and his perjury and treason were against you. On this ground I call for his execution, and will back this plea with my sword.' The Franks declare that what he says is right. But Pinabel comes forward to dispute Thierry's case and seek combat with him. His thirty kinsmen will stand surety for Ganelon. The King accepts his glove and Thierry's, then has four benches carried to the place of combat for those about to fight. The others accept their challenges as fair; and with Ogier of Denmark ensuring that the proper forms are observed, they call for horses and arms. When the combatants have been confessed and shriven, heard Mass, and placed great offerings in the churches, they come before Charles to arm and mount their steeds. A hundred thousand knights weep, pitying Thierry for Roland's sake. God in His wisdom knows how the judgement will fall.

The combat is held in a wide meadow below Aix. It takes the same course as the fight between Charlemagne and Baligant: the contestants are unhorsed, then continue their struggle on foot. 'Oh God', cries Charles, 'make it plain where justice lies!' Pinabel calls on Thierry to yield, promising him much wealth and his own service, if he will make Ganelon's peace with the King. Thierry refuses: let God show who is in the right. But if Pinabel will stop fighting, he will reconcile him with Charlemagne, though such justice will be taken on Ganelon as will be talked about for evermore. Pinabel will have none of it, and they smite on, striking such fire from their helmets that the grass is kindled. A blow from Pinabel cuts across Thierry's face and through his hauberk. His blood falls bright on the meadow grass, but God spares his life. With his own sword, he splits his opponent's helmet down to the nasal, cleaving his head and spilling out the brains. With this single stroke the combat is won; and the outcome is acclaimed by the Franks as a miraculous verdict on Ganelon.

Plate 78

Charlemagne comes to embrace Thierry and wipes his face with his own fur cape, donning another in its place. Then, gently disarming the knight, they lead him back in triumph to Aix. The Emperor appeals to his barons: 'What should I do with those thirty hostages who came here to support Ganelon?'—'Let none remain alive', is the reply. So Charles commands his provost to have them all hanged on the gallows-tree. His orders are executed without delay. 'Traitors work their own deaths and others' too' is the poet's grim comment.

Plate 79 Then, on the Franks' insistence that Ganelon should die in agony, four mettlesome chargers are brought, to which he is bound by hands and feet. The horses, goaded and urged by serving-men, rush towards a stream that flows across a field. There Ganelon meets his end with every nerve and sinew snapped, his limbs smashed and torn apart, his bright blood spreading over the green grass. In this way he dies a felon's death: a traitor should not live to boast of his deed!

When the Emperor's justice is done, he summons together the bishops of Bavaria, Germany, and France, saying he holds a noble captive who has been won by sermons and parables to the Christian faith. So, amid a great throng in the baths at Aix, the Queen of Spain receives baptism, exchanging the name of Bramimonde for that of Juliane. That night the Emperor lies in his vaulted chamber, when the angel Gabriel comes to him, bearing word from God that he must assemble his armies once again and go to aid King Vivien in Imphe in the land of Bire, where he is beset by infidels. 'Oh God,' says noble Charlemagne, 'how weary my life is!' His eyes fill with tears, and he plucks at his white beard. 'Here ends the story Turoldus completes.'

75 'As far as Blaye he brings his nephew back
And his companion, noble Oliver,
And the Archbishop, that wise, worthy man.
He has the barons in white coffins laid;
And there the lords still lie in Saint Romain.'
(ll. 3689–93)

76–XIX (Overleaf) The funeral of Roland and the death of Aude in Charlemagne's arms. ▶

76

XIX

77 (Above)

> 'Now the case starts and the trial begins
> Of Ganelon, who worked the treachery.
> He is dragged forth before the Emperor.'
> (ll. 3747–9)

78 (Left) Single combat between Ganelon's champion Pinabel and Thierry, fighting for Charles:

> 'Down below Aix a spacious meadow lies:
> There the two barons' combat is engaged.'
> (ll. 3873–4)

Comment guennelon conte de champaigne
fu iugie a morir honteusement par les prin
ces et barons de la court du bon charlemaine

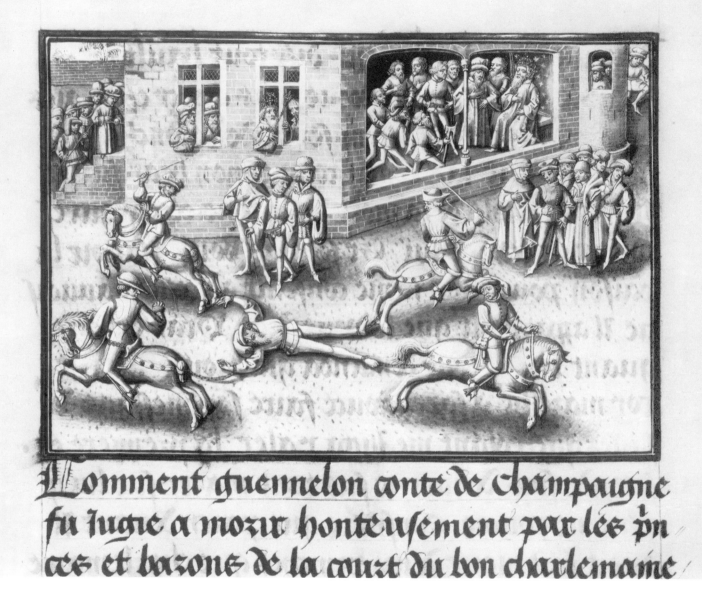

79 The trial of Ganelon before Charles in a 'mansion' like the medieval stage, and below, the execution, as the Emperor watches from a window and the court queue for places. Some spectators are even scaling the boundary wall at the back.

80–81 This bronze equestrian statue has been traditionally identified as Charlemagne, though this is by no means uncontested, and it may represent his grandson Charles the Bald. The horse is a Renaissance restoration. The figure is dressed as Einhard describes Charles (see p. 21, above). Probably the best portrait of the Emperor is to be found on the silver deniers minted in the last year of his reign, the reverse of which bear a symbolic representation of the Church. Later generations were to turn his defence of the Empire against the Moors into a religious crusade.

The Later Legends

In the Song of Roland we find reference to numerous events in the hero's earlier career: the taking of Noples, for instance, presumably his past destruction of the citadel of Galne, and certainly his many conquests in the service of Charlemagne, ranging from Scotland to Constantinople. If we are to believe Ganelon, his behaviour had not always lived up to the highest traditions of Christian chivalry; and indeed it is even conceded by Thierry that he may have wronged his stepfather in the past. Be that as it may, it seems more than possible that at the time of the Oxford text more stories were circulating about him than are reported there. But in any case, what a splendid opportunity was now presented to the forgers of legend, who found themselves with an illustrious hero in need of a detailed poetic biography. So they set to work piecemeal, it appears, and did what they could. To tell when or by whom this or that episode was invented would be a hard and often hopeless task, however; and in the following pages I shall merely look briefly at some of the main happenings in what will be treated as a progressively evolving career.

I have already mentioned the dark mystery surrounding Roland's birth; but it was no mystery for the poet who composed, in a Franco-Italian dialect, the song of *Berta e Milone.* This tells of Charlemagne's sister Bertha and how one day, while he was out hunting, she escaped his watchful *Plate 82* eye and gave herself to Milo, a knight of modest breeding. In time, finding she was to have a child, she fled with her lover to Italy and lived there with him in great hardship. Their wanderings took them to a cave near Imola, and in this humble refuge their son Roland was born. Fearing for the child's safety (the poet draws parallels with the birth and childhood of Christ), they chose to move to a forest not far from Rome, where Milo worked as a woodcutter. There, according to another poem, Charles came across the fugitives by chance and at once felt an instinctive love for his nephew. The lovers were pardoned, and Roland was later privileged to attend his parents' wedding.

82 The Roland story was known on the Italian pilgrimage routes. At Borgo San Donnino a sculptured frieze shows a legend not contained in the *Chanson de Roland*: the love of Charlemagne's sister Bertha for Count Milo and Roland's birth as the result of their union. Banished by Charles, Milo supported his family by woodcutting; on the left, young Roland follows his father into the forest.

83 Young Roland won his spurs by saving Charlemagne's life in a battle with Eaumont, a heathen king (see also Plate 14). He is brandishing a stick, the ignoble weapon he used before winning Durendal in this, his first fight. Naimes and Ogier ride behind him.

XX (Overleaf) Divine intervention halts the combat between the equally-matched Roland and Oliver beneath the walls of Vienne. ▶

par auant lui auoit este donne du duc rolant.

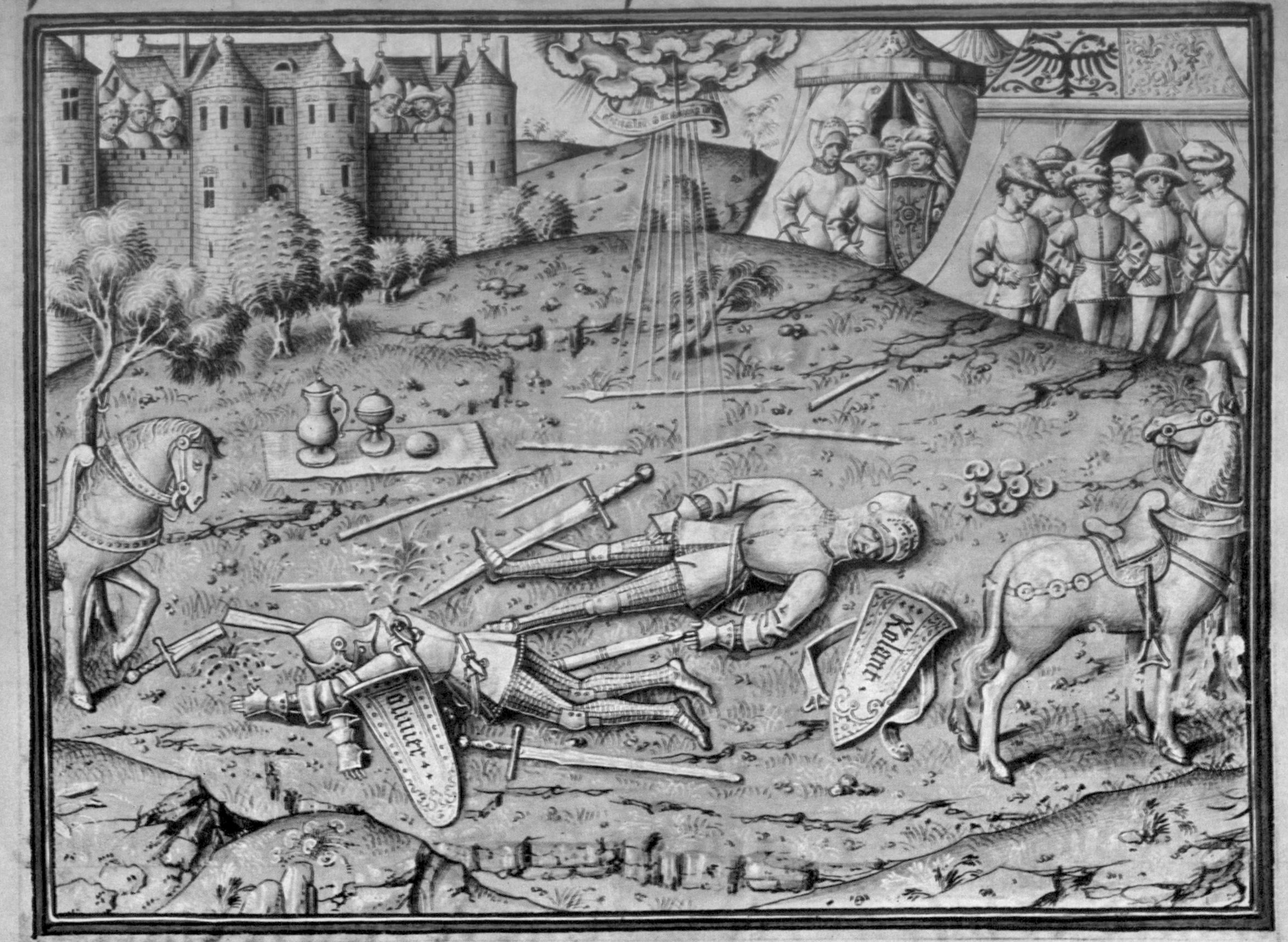

Cõment langle de nostreseigneur visitta et pacifia roland et oliuier de leur different. Et cõment rolant racompta a Charlemaine sa visi

Listoire contient que les deux vaillans vassaulx gesans par terre lun empres lautre comme gens endormis ou sans aucune vie furent longuement

Brought up in the royal household, the boy very soon showed his mettle. One day Charles had news from Italy of the aggression of a pagan king, Agolant. At once he set out with his army, leaving Roland and three companions shut in the fortress of Laon, since they were too young to fight. But the lads escaped on stolen horses and made their way to Italy, where the Franks were engaged in a great battle at Aspremont. Charles himself was hard pressed by Eaumont, son of the pagan king; but in the nick of time Roland arrived brandishing a stick as his only weapon. *Plate 83* He saved his uncle's life by slaying Eaumont; and from his victim he seized his oliphant, the sword Durendal, and the charger Veillantif. In gratitude, once the battle was over, Charles dubbed him knight in Eaumont's own tent. Roland later engaged in a victorious combat against King *Plates 84–86* Agolant himself. The young hero has now truly won his spurs.

But he has not yet found his companion Oliver; and this turning-point in his life of chivalry *Plate 87* is recounted in *Girart de Vienne*. From time to time in the pages of epic, Charlemagne was plagued by revolts among his vassals (and, to be honest, the initial fault was not always on their side). So it happened that Duke Girart, who, before he had obtained his fief of Vienne, had spent some time at the royal court, took offence at some affront suffered from the Emperor and his queen, and as a result, war broke out between them. With Girart in Vienne were his brother Renier and the latter's two children, Oliver and the beautiful Aude; and when Charles came with his army to besiege the city, Oliver would climb with his sister onto the battlements to watch the preparations that were afoot. One day Roland, already an honoured member of his uncle's company, was hunting with a falcon outside the city, when the bird flew off in the wrong direction and was taken by Oliver up there on the walls. As Roland watched the falcon's flight, his eye lit on Aude, that paragon of maidens, and his heart was at once ensnared.

The incident and the ensuing events are depicted in a single scene by Jean le Tavernier, who *Plate 88* was illustrating the story as found in a later prose chronicle. Roland made for the walls, swinging his hunting-glove to show he had no hostile intent, and called to Aude to ask her brother to return the bird to him. This Aude did; and Oliver duly rode out of the city to hand it over with all courtesy. However, Girart's nephew, Aimery de Beaulande, felt it wrong to let the nephew of the Emperor himself go off again without a challenge. Though Roland's thoughts were now more on love than on martial exercise, he was forced to fight, while Aude and Oliver looked on from their vantage-point. But the affair ended well, with Aimery being both unhorsed and spared by his vanquisher.

Untypically, but understandably, Roland's heart is not in the seven-year siege of Vienne. But fight he must; and another grisaille shows him with Charlemagne in a skirmish, while Oliver

◄ XX

Plate 89 appears fighting with a stick, a mode of combat that Roland was to disapprove at Roncevaux. At length it is decided that the matter must be settled by a single combat between two champions; *Plate* XX and that honour is granted to Roland and Oliver by their respective uncles. To the dismay and emotional confusion of the watching Aude, who reciprocates Roland's tender feelings, the evenly matched duel seems to drag on for ever. At God's bidding, however, an angel finally intervenes to separate the combatants, for they are destined to live on to face their greatest trial against the Saracens in Spain. They vow to make peace between their uncles; but their good intentions are not realized, and the war continues. When eventually, with Charlemagne at his mercy, Girart has *Plates 90, 91* a sudden change of heart and begs forgiveness, the betrothal of Aude and Roland is arranged. But before the ceremony has been concluded, messengers bring word that the Spanish infidels have invaded France: the Emperor has a new war on his hands.

Girart de Vienne was not the only vassal to give Charlemagne trouble, as I have said. The four sons of Aymon de Dordone, for instance, were a painful thorn in his flesh. Outlawed, they built their own castle of Montauban, and there had to suffer his siege. In their cousin Maugis, they found an invaluable ally. Combining the roles of knight, bandit, and magician, he was a diffi- *Plates 92,* XXI cult man to deal with. Once he was captured by Oliver and taken before the Emperor. Charles invited him to supper, but tempered his hospitality with the assurance that he was to die the following day. This by no means suited the crafty Maugis, who proceeded to put Charles and his peers into a kind of trance, able to hear, but not to speak or stir a finger. This done, he relieved them of their swords, including Joyeuse and Durendal, and carried his impudence to the length of absconding with the royal crown as well. On another occasion he transported the spell-bound Charlemagne into Montauban itself. But it is a long story, and we must leave it there.

Roland, as can be seen, did not always figure as the proudly conquering hero; and he can be found in humiliating circumstances even in his dealings with the infidels. A pagan king, Balan *Plate 93* (or Laban), sacked Rome and was pursued into Spain by the Franks, with Oliver in particular performing glorious deeds. In a series of combats there, all of the peers were captured by Balan and imprisoned in his dungeons. Fortunately for them, the King's daughter succumbed to the charms of their comrade Gui de Bourgogne; and she gave the captives precious help until they were delivered by Charlemagne, and Balan was decapitated.

If Roland cuts a sorry figure in Jean le Tavernier's picture of him and his companion being hustled before the hirsute King Balan, he appears in a more characteristic attitude in Loyset *Plate 94* Liédet's miniature, which shows him mounted on the splendid Veillantif at the head of the whole army, as he spears to death a Saracen before Charlemagne's somewhat impassive gaze. Now

84 Naimes and Ogier have told Charles of Roland's desire to be knighted. In Eaumont's tent, uncle embraces nephew in a tender gesture of affection.

85 To do honour to his nephew, Charlemagne holds a ceremonial knighting; here he is girding on the swords of several sons of dukes and peers.

Coment le noble Charlemaine ordonna ses batailles
pour combatre les payens. Et coment le saint pere
ottroia a turpin larcevesque de porter ce jour la croix
Istoire contient que quant le noble

86 The first exploit of Roland, the newly-made knight: protected by three haloed saints, the oliphant hanging from his shoulder, he strikes the first blow in a fight with a heathen king; meanwhile Ogier the Dane looks on in the background. In the right foreground, the Pope is entrusting the True Cross to Turpin.

87 Durendal at the ready, young Roland on his prancing horse rides out in search of adventure.

XXI In the *chanson* of *Renaut de Montauban,* the crafty enchanter Maugis gets the better of Charlemagne and his peers. He places them under a spell and steals their swords.

Comment rolant et oliuier sentrecongneu
rent et acointerent premierement ensemble
Et comment aimery de beaulande iousta contre
rolant et fu abatu deuant la belle aude · ꝛc.

88 At the siege of Vienne, Roland's hawk flies off and is captured by Oliver, standing on the walls with his sister Aude. Oliver courteously returns it, but Roland is challenged by Aimery de Beaulande, whom he defeats but spares. Each detail of the grisaille closely follows *Girart de Vienne.*

Comment le noble empereur et le duc rolat
se rebouterent en la bataille.
Le noble duc veant son oncle arme
et mis en point se partir du tref

89 The siege drags on. In this engagement, Roland (top right) defeats and spares his adversary while in the foreground a gigantic Oliver brandishes the club with which he is often shown. The siege will not end until the two champions have met face to face (see Plate XX, above).

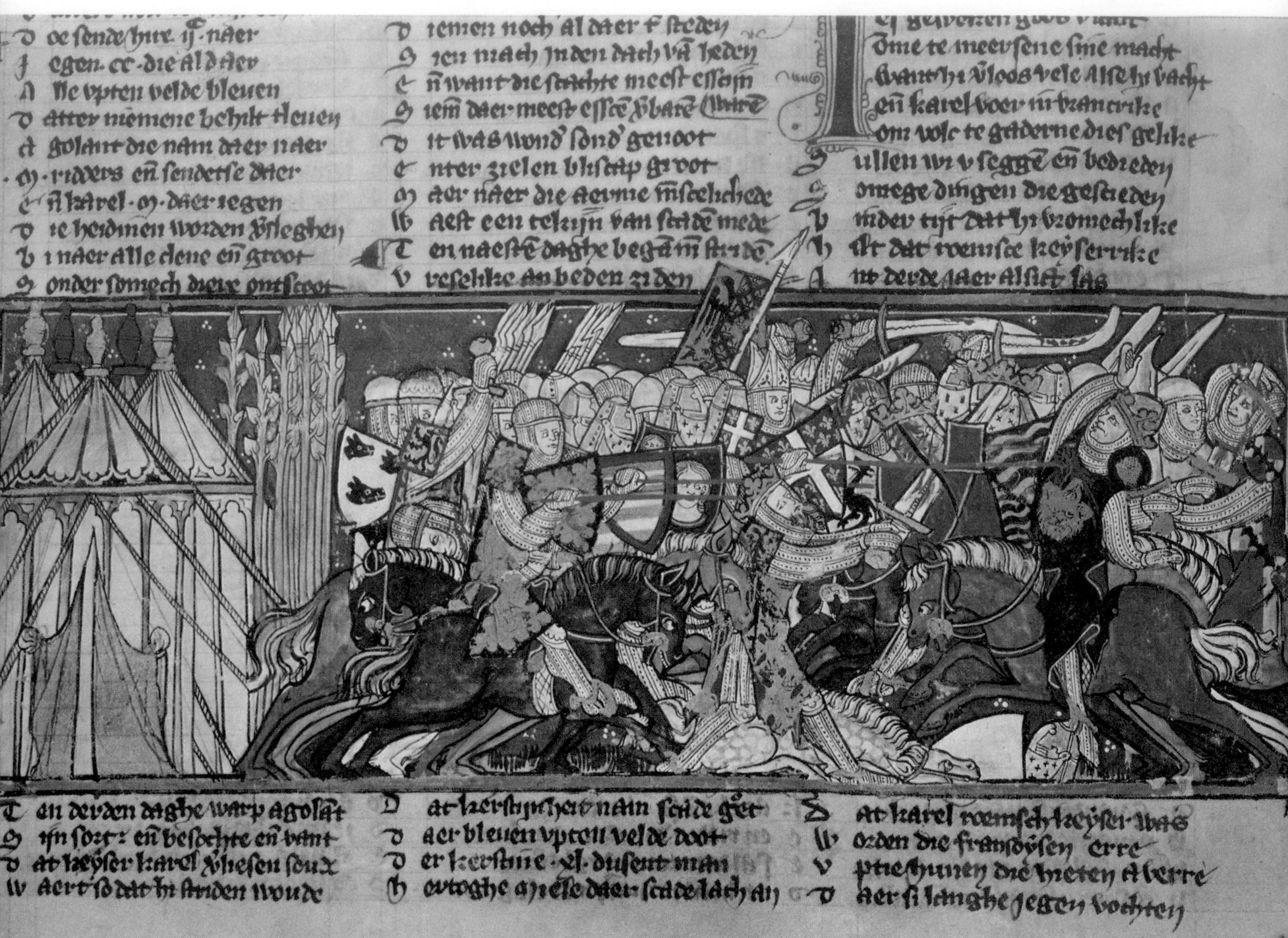

XXII After the miracle of the flowering lances (see also above, Plate IV) came the battle with Agolant. Charlemagne, hard pressed, has been unhorsed, but Roland and the peers come to the rescue. Agolant then withdrew and captured Agen.

Comment les grans oſtz de lempereur cha
lemaine ſaſſamblerent au iour deuant dit
pour aler conquerir les eſpaignes / &c.

90 The appearance of Aude in the Roland story is rare. Oliver's sister was first seen by Roland at the siege of Vienne; eventually the lovers were betrothed, but the army was then already marshalling for the fateful Spanish campaign.

le contraire de ce qui estoit veritable.
Comment le puissant empereur ala au
deuant du noble duc gerard de vienne et
de sa niepce aude la suer du conte oliuier.

91 Anxious because of a prophetic dream, Aude and her father Girart de Vienne come to ask Charlemagne for news of Roland. Behind stand the walls of Blaye, for the tragedy of Roncevaux is almost played out and the heroes will lie in the church of St. Romain.

92 Having caſt Charlemagne and his knights into an enchanted sleep, Maugis ſtrips them of their swords, which he then takes to Montauban.

Comment maulgis daigremont endormy char
lemaine et ses barons par nigromance et si
emporta leurs espees en montauban

Or dist listoire que quant lempereur
eut fait lier maulgis a ung piller
et quil eut soupe Il fist lors ses barons venir
entour lui et leur dist quil convenoit

93 Roland is not always shown in the best light. Defeated and captured by the Saracens, he and the peers were imprisoned until their rescue by Charlemagne. The bearded King Balan is a magnificent Oriental figure with his heavy bejewelled turban.

clouds of glory gather ever brighter around him as he leaves behind the days of youthful irresponsibility when a glance from Aude would fire him as much as the glint of pagan arms. With his uncle he undertakes the pilgrimage to Jerusalem; and it appears to be he whom we see with Charles devoutly kneeling before the True Cross. Before long he will be riding with the Frankish armies on their fateful campaign beyond the Pyrenees. *Plate 95*

It is the *Pseudo-Turpin Chronicle* that tells us most of what happened there. A great deal of the action is foreign to the *Song of Roland*, whilst the events common to both are told more cursorily, but with new detail, some of it clashing with the poet's version. Yet, as I said earlier, this is the account which, in the original Latin or in vernacular redactions, guided the hands of the illustrators most strongly.

The first pagan citadel to fall to Charlemagne was Pamplona. For three months it held out against his siege; then the King dropped to his knees and prayed to God and St. James to help him. The miracle of Jericho was repeated, for the walls crumbled, and the city lay open to the Franks. The pagans who accepted Christianity were baptized, the rest put to the sword. Many other Saracen strongholds were taken, among them the city of Luiserne, when Charles, with the authority of a Moses, commanded that it be engulfed beneath the waters. After three years he returned to France and there built many churches. *Plate 96* *Plate 97*

Then there came news that an African king, Agolant (the namesake of Charles's foe in the *Aspremont* story), had conquered Spain from the Christians left to defend it. Again the Emperor mustered an army and marched south, with Duke Milo, Roland's father, as his chief in command. Agolant was encountered and a series of combats engaged, each involving a greater number of Christians and pagans. The two kings agreed that the following day they would commit their whole armies to battle. That night some of the Franks thrust their lances into the ground in front of their tents; and when morning came, it was found that they had grown bark and leaves. The knights cut them off at the ground; and from the roots they left sprang groves, which may still be seen. In the ensuing battle Duke Milo was slain, along with many Christians who owned the sprouting lances. Charlemagne himself was in great peril, for with his horse killed beneath him, he was forced to fight on foot, wielding his sword to great effect against the encircling heathens. Next day, however, Christian reinforcements arrived: Agolant fled, and Charles was able to return to France. *Plates IV, XXII*

This was still not the end of the matter, for Agolant gathered another great host and seized the city of Agen in Gascony. Negotiations were opened, with a singular lack of good faith on both sides; but it was left to the Emperor to reduce the town by a six-month siege. He entered *Plate 98* it to find the chief infidels gone, although ten thousand pagans were left to be slaughtered *Plate 99* by the Franks. The war continued until Agolant made his final stand in the restored Pamplona. There the contest was pursued with homily and argument as well as sharp steel, and at one moment Agolant was even on the point of espousing Christianity. Yet in the end it was the usual full-scale battle that decided where the right lay: by its close, Agolant had been slain with all but a handful of the Saracens.

Although in these Spanish adventures we are to think of Roland as playing only a supporting role, in the next act the star part is his. The Christians are suddenly confronted by a new and even greater menace in the shape of a giant, Ferragut, who has been sent by the Emir of Babylon (or Cairo) with a vast army of Turks. Though Ferragut's immense size was calculated to inspire dread *Plate 101* in his foes, the medieval illustrators took him to their hearts and depicted his deeds often and with apparent relish. When faced by Charlemagne, Ferragut calls for single combats, and with good reason; for Ogier of Denmark, the first to be sent against him, is picked up without ceremony and carried off under his arm into captivity. Another follows, and then they come two by two, all receiving the same treatment until a score of Charles's knights are safely in the giant's prison.

The Emperor fears to send more of his Christians to undergo this degrading treatment, but in answer to Roland's entreaties he finally allows him to go and try his chance. It seems that Char- *Plate 100* les's nephew will have little more success than the others, for Ferragut picks him up in one hand *Plates 102, 103* and sets him on his horse. Roland, however, contrives to grasp the giant by the chin and up-end him, both of them falling to the ground. Remounting, they begin a fierce combat in which first their steeds are slain, then their swords lost; but they continue to belabour each other with fists and stones until darkness falls. After a night's truce they resume their duel with various weapons and either mounted or on foot (there are different versions of the events). Then at noon Fer- *Plate 104* ragut feels weary, and Roland grants him a further truce so that he can sleep for a while, even placing a stone under his head for greater comfort.

When the giant wakes, Roland asks him about his remarkable invulnerability to all types of weapons. With curious naivety, Ferragut gives the information that he can be killed only by a thrust through the navel. An ensuing dispute as to whether Islam or Christianity is the true religion might be thought superfluous in the circumstances, especially when the opposing theological arguments fail to produce any weakening of resolves; and so once more they resort to fighting, having agreed that the one who gains victory will have established the superiority of his own faith. With his sword, or in some accounts the giant's own dagger, Roland seeks out his

La bataille de charlemaine alencontre de agoulant
Et de Jaumont son filz et dautres faiz.
Bien auez ouy dessus cõment Charlemaine
roy de france fu couronne a empereur par
la main de pape lion en la cite de romme.

94 Roland, at the head of the army, is acting as Charlemagne's champion, mounted on a splendidly caparisoned Veillantif. He strikes down a pagan king with his lance. The realistically painted heavy war-horses are typical of the age in which the miniature was painted, if not of the age of Charlemagne, and compare favourably with Jean Le Tavernier's prancing hobby-horses.

95 Roland and Charlemagne were even credited with a pilgrimage to Jerusalem; they are shown adoring the True Cross.

96 The first Christian success in the Spanish Campaign was the capture of Pamplona, which fell when the Lord answered Charlemagne's prayers with the same miracle He had worked for Joshua before the walls of Jericho. The figure holding the shield with the Imperial arms in the left foreground is Roland, Charles's sword-bearer.

97 Another Old Testament miracle was repeated in the Spanish War: Charles stands like Moses, and at his command, the waters engulf the heathen city of Luiserne. His knights stand behind him in judicial robes.

98 Charlemagne, riding at the head of his knights, his charger decked with the arms of France and the Empire, is marching on the Saracen-held town of Agen which he will capture after a six-month siege.

99 After the various sieges and engagements of the war in Spain, the conflict with Agolant was resolved by a full-scale battle, ending in Christian triumph. In the small scenes at the top of this miniature is Charlemagne's coronation, as King of France and Emperor. The funeral below is his.

100 (Opposite) Roland played a leading part in the conflict with Ferragut, the giant champion of Islam, who first carried him off across his horse. ▸

Por ele eschiuast sil pouist uos eterre.
Por grant dotange. Roll'. le frenis sacha.
Le bō destrer, qe le freis redota.
Le chief le piez les piz deuant dreça.
Le colp de fust lo destrer asena.
Par mié le chief dū lestr sparagna.
Quāt chil auūt de tōt esbrisa.
Oilz e cerueles aual en trabuca.
E les balotes dotinel auaqoi.
Les dos greignors le bō cheual frapa.
Le neueu Carles la tere tristona.
Si sor le flanch que dagose pasma.
Le cheual chiet que mort 7 demora.
Roll'. sen broche sor le mort che uersa.
Pasmez stordiz de piece nō leua.
Tant aua leist. Feragu. sachina.
Croit qe mort soit par les flans le cobra.
Sor son cheual le mist e trausa.

Le petit pas uers la cite torna.
Se cil nō panse qe le mort susita.

101–102 First Ferragut (above, far left) captures two Christian knights and takes them off to his castle. Then Roland, championing the Christian side, challenges him. Their struggle follows the same course in most manuscripts: the combat is at first mounted, with lances or swords. Sometimes Ferragut, as befits a pagan, wields a flail (opposite). This engagement proving indecisive, a *disputoison* ensues, a form of debate in which Roland endeavours to convert his adversary by his arguments. The gestures of the adversaries as each makes his point are typical of representations of medieval scholars in debate.

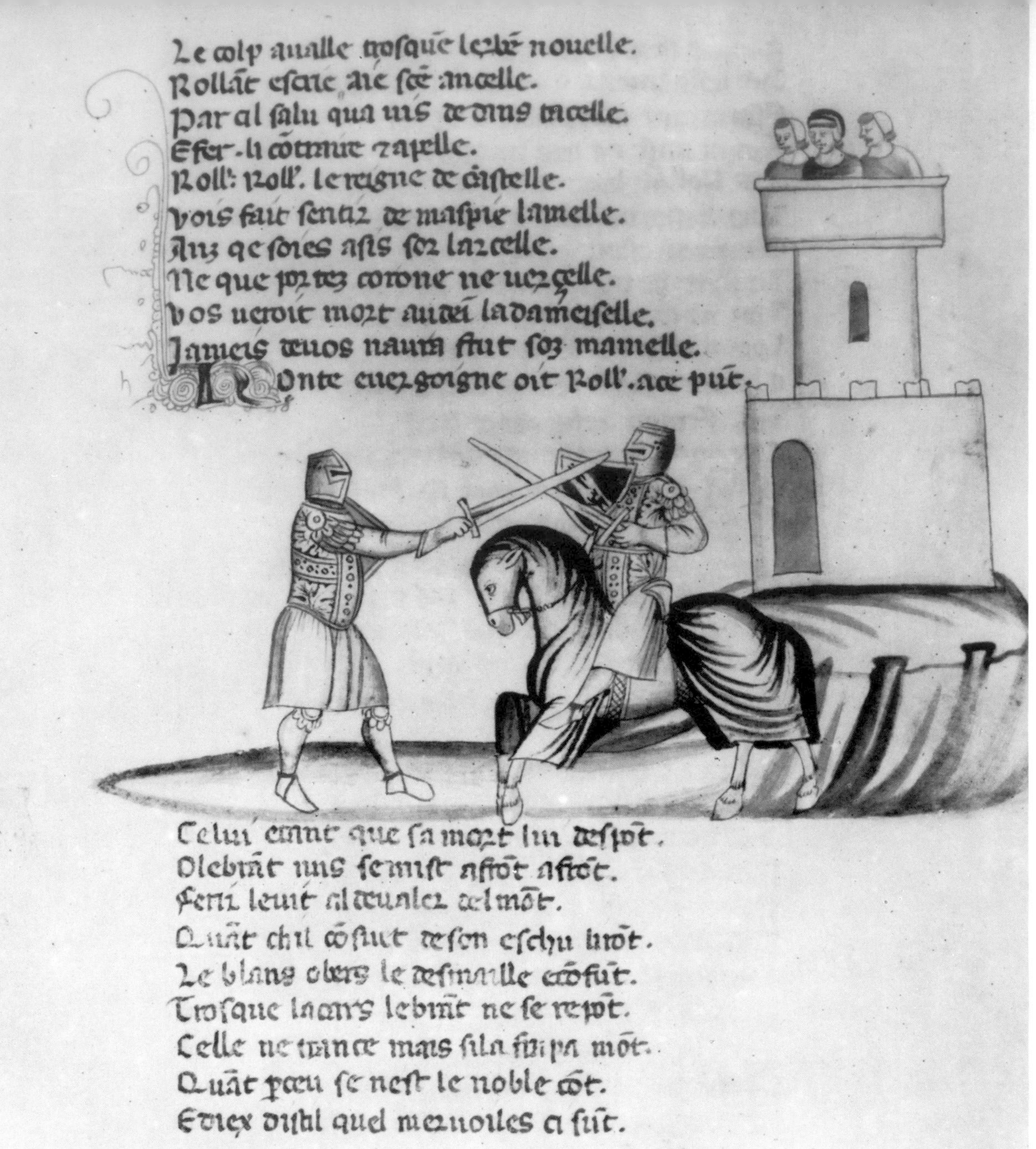

103–104 The fight continues. Eventually Roland's horse is killed beneath him and as the Christians watch from the walls of Nájera, he sets about Ferragut with his sword. By the end of that day, Ferragut is weary, and with his customary chivalry, Roland places a stone under Ferragut's head as a pillow so he may rest.

64

De soz son braç tient le chief amasis.
Si fort soz voille come fust ũ fol mis.
R. loi si dist par sant tomais.
Je croi qil dort cist fil de satanis
En cele part sen vient a petit pais.
Prist un perõ chil voit elegans.
Se dunc vousist nel tenez mie a gais.
Oncas oust le turch en es le pis.
Mais nel ferot par tot lor de bauduis.

Li chief li leve sens mal 7 sens forfais.
E par tant al nese veille pais.
Mist li la piere pues avit el testis.
Or vole bië ertoi de cors vertus.
Chis de lignaie al iaiãt Golias.
Con cist david de son sant de tolais.
De sol troi pieres el plans de chalois.
Le cors mi dist qe tu nõ estordirais.
Caton ancestre hoi cõpaigne ferais.
Or te de mort que nõ leuas tu mais.
Quãt en sant font batiez nesfis.

Comment le duc rolant conquist vng iaiād
terrible nomme fernagud et conquist nadres
la grant cite et de ses emprises

105 Ferragut unwisely reveals that his one vulnerable spot is his navel and the fight is ended when Roland strikes him there. This grisaille contains several elements of the story telescoped together: on the left, the giant is bearing off two small knights, kicking and screaming, to the Saracen camp. In the foreground the two chargers lie dead.

adversary's vulnerable spot, and Ferragut is slain. The Christians break into the city of Nájera, where these events have taken place, and liberate their imprisoned comrades. *Plate 105*

In the *Entrée d'Espagne*, one of the later epics, Roland leave Nájera for the siege of Pamplona. There, finding the action not brisk enough for his taste, he decides that more glory is to be won by liberating Noples (Noble) from the infidels. With the other peers he secretly leaves Pamplona to accomplish the feat of which Ganelon so scathingly reminded Charles in the *Song of Roland*. When he returns in triumph to the Emperor after his exploit of a single day, he is met with unexpected coldness; for by his absence, unapproved by his uncle, he has added years to the duration of the siege. In his anger, Charles strikes him with his iron gauntlet, drawing blood. With considerable self-control, Roland leaves the Emperor's tent and rides in anger from the camp. *Plate 106* (See *Plate* VIII) *Plates 107,* XXIII

He makes for the coast, where he takes ship for the East. There he has many adventures under an assumed name, and a last brush with romance. For in Persia the Sultan's beautiful daughter falls in love with him, and he undertakes to free her from an unwanted suitor. He wins his duel to the plaudits of the court and in the presence of the Sultan and the girl; but remaining faithful to Aude, he leaves the fair princess to be married to Anseïs de Blois, and himself makes his way back to Spain, to Charlemagne and Oliver, and before long to Roncevaux. *Plates 108–9*

The *Pseudo-Turpin Chronicle* introduces us to Marsile and Baligant as two Saracen kings subject to Charlemagne. But hearing that their loyalty is suspect, the Emperor sends Ganelon to require that they be baptized or pay tribute. Then the familiar treason is accomplished and its consequences seen. The rearguard's defeat is explained by the fact that among the pagans' gifts had been a quantity of wine, which some of the French had enjoyed to excess. In their drunkenness they had slept with women, among whom were both Saracens and some Christians who had come with the army from France. In the great battle the whole rearguard perished save Roland, his stepbrother Baldwin, Turpin, Thierry, and a few others, such was the punishment brought by the guilty on themselves and on the innocent too. (See *Plate 23*)

With the main action lost, Roland came across a black pagan hiding in a grove. Seizing the heathen, he tied him to a tree, then climbed a hill to see the position of the enemy troops. He blew his horn, and about a hundred Christian survivors rallied to him. With them he returned to his captive, unbound him, and took him to a spot from which the Saracens could be seen. Roland then forced the pagan to point out Marsile. The small band charged into the enemy ranks and, now sure of his man, Roland made an end of their leader. Learning of Marsile's death, Baligant fled the country. *Plate 110*

The men who had made this last sally with Roland had been slain and he himself gravely wounded. Now he tries to break Durendal and only now to summon Charles by blowing the *Plate 111* oliphant. As he lies dying, Baldwin appears. Roland asks him to fetch water, but there is none to be found (in other versions some is in fact produced); and afraid lest he should fall into Saracen hands, Baldwin gives his blessing and rides off to join Charles and the army. When he has gone, Thierry passes that way. Finding Roland near to death, he hears the hero's last con- *Plates 21, 112* fession before angels come to bear away his noble soul.

At that moment Turpin was saying Mass before Charlemagne, when he had a vision of demons carrying Marsile to Hell and St. Michael bearing Roland and the other Christian heroes to Heaven. After the service, he was telling Charles of this when Baldwin (or Thierry) arrived with the full story of the disaster at Roncevaux. The army hastened back to the pass, where Charles found his nephew's corpse to his great grief; and in the morning they discovered the body of his companion Oliver, flayed, mutilated, and crucified. The Emperor's revenge on the Saracens and Ganelon is much the same as in the Song.

Plate 113 A legend not carried in the *Chronicle* tells that on his return to Roncevaux Charlemagne had prayed for a miracle to enable him to distinguish the Christian dead from the heathen. Immediately briars sprang from the bodies of the pagans, while the French were covered with hawthorn flowers (or lilies). The later writers have indeed gone to great pains to convince us that the Oxford poet put no idle words into the mouth of the good Archibishop when he promised that all who died in battle would secure divine approval and the joys of Paradise. Even on earth they lay amid celestial flowers.

In these more devout accounts of Roncevaux, Roland himself has taken on an aura of saintliness which his conduct in the Song might be supposed scarcely to merit. Yet this is an ungenerous thought; for a hero is probably more admirable and certainly more interesting if he has human imperfections above which he can rise. About the actual military leader who fought and died for the mighty Frankish king in that lonely Pyrenean pass we can know nothing. But out *Plate* XXIV of his memory the men of France, and not only of France, have fashioned a figure that speaks *Plates 114, 115* eloquently of their own ideals of courage, honour, and loyalty to a cause. Who then would deny to Roland his place with Charlemagne in Dante's Paradise, or challenge his right to stand guard with Oliver, his dear companion, over the pilgrim route that crosses the Pyrenees to St. James's shrine in Spain?

106 An incident in the battle for Pamplona from *L'Entrée d'Espagne*, one of the finest illustrated manuscripts of the Spanish Campaign.

107–XXIII Having slipped away from the siege of Pamplona to capture Noples in one day (see Plate VIII, above), Roland returns in triumph to Charlemagne. But the Emperor, enraged at this absence without leave, strikes Roland on the face with his gauntlet. The hero leaves camp and rides out, a solitary figure, to seek adventures in the East.

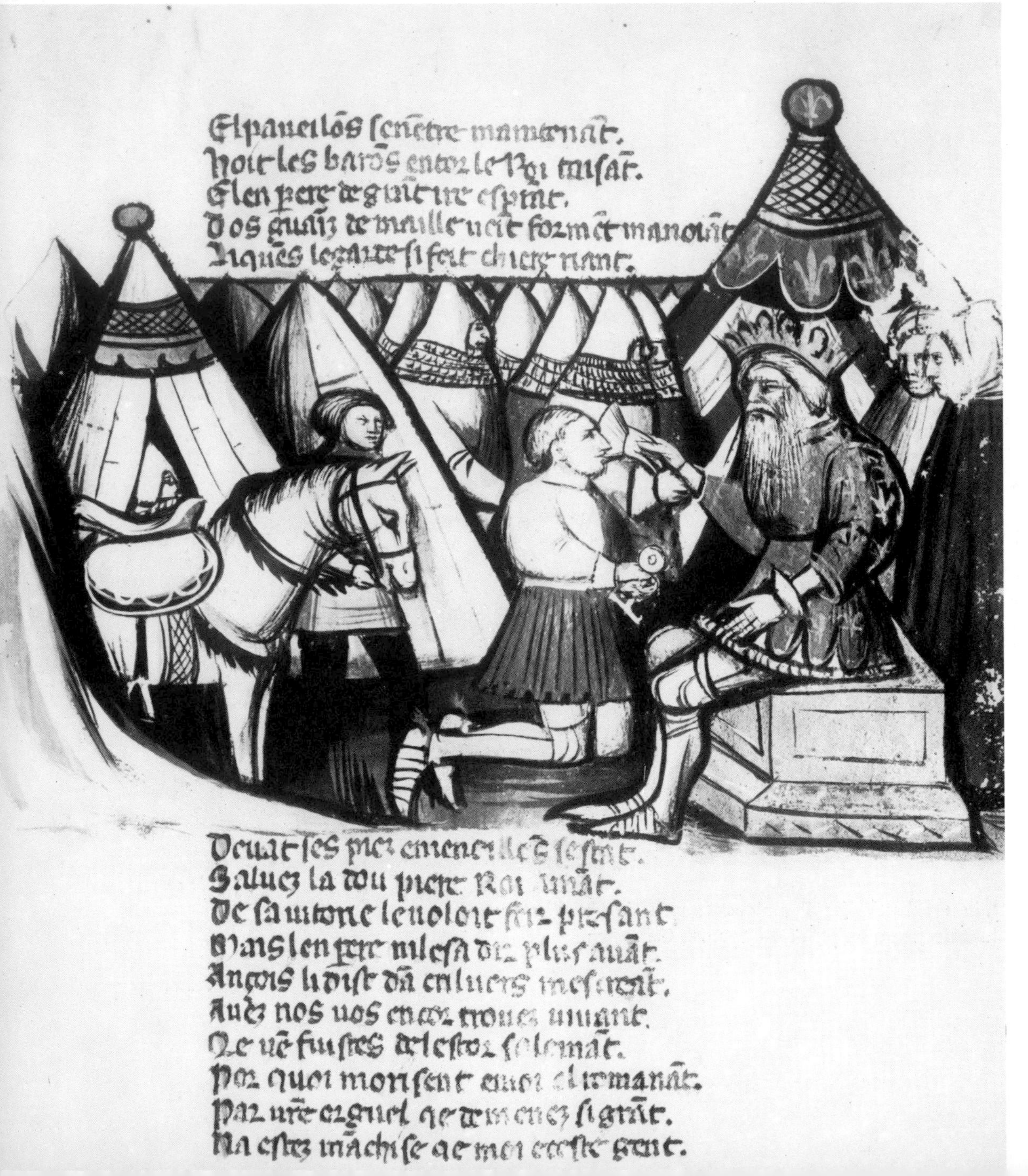

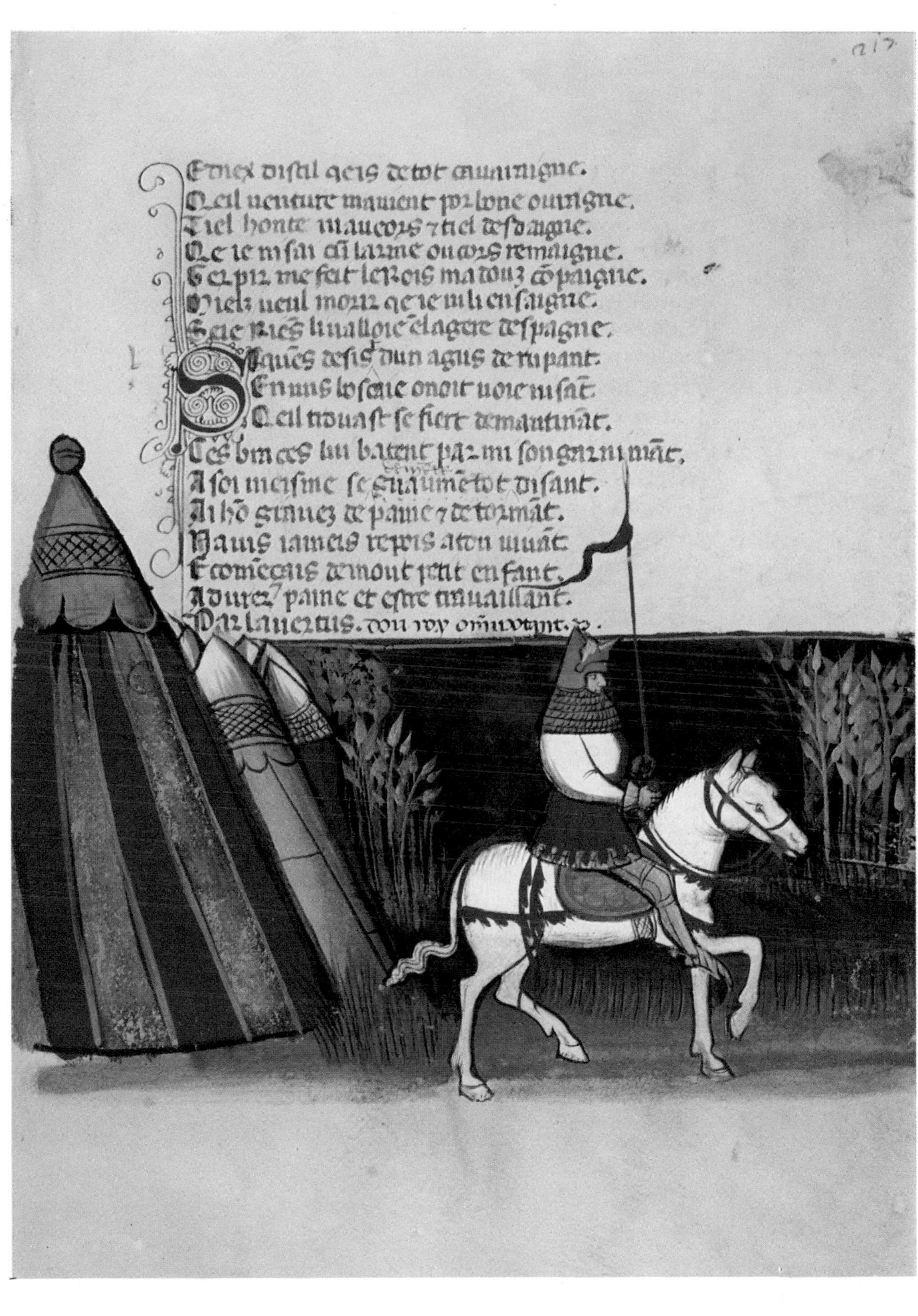

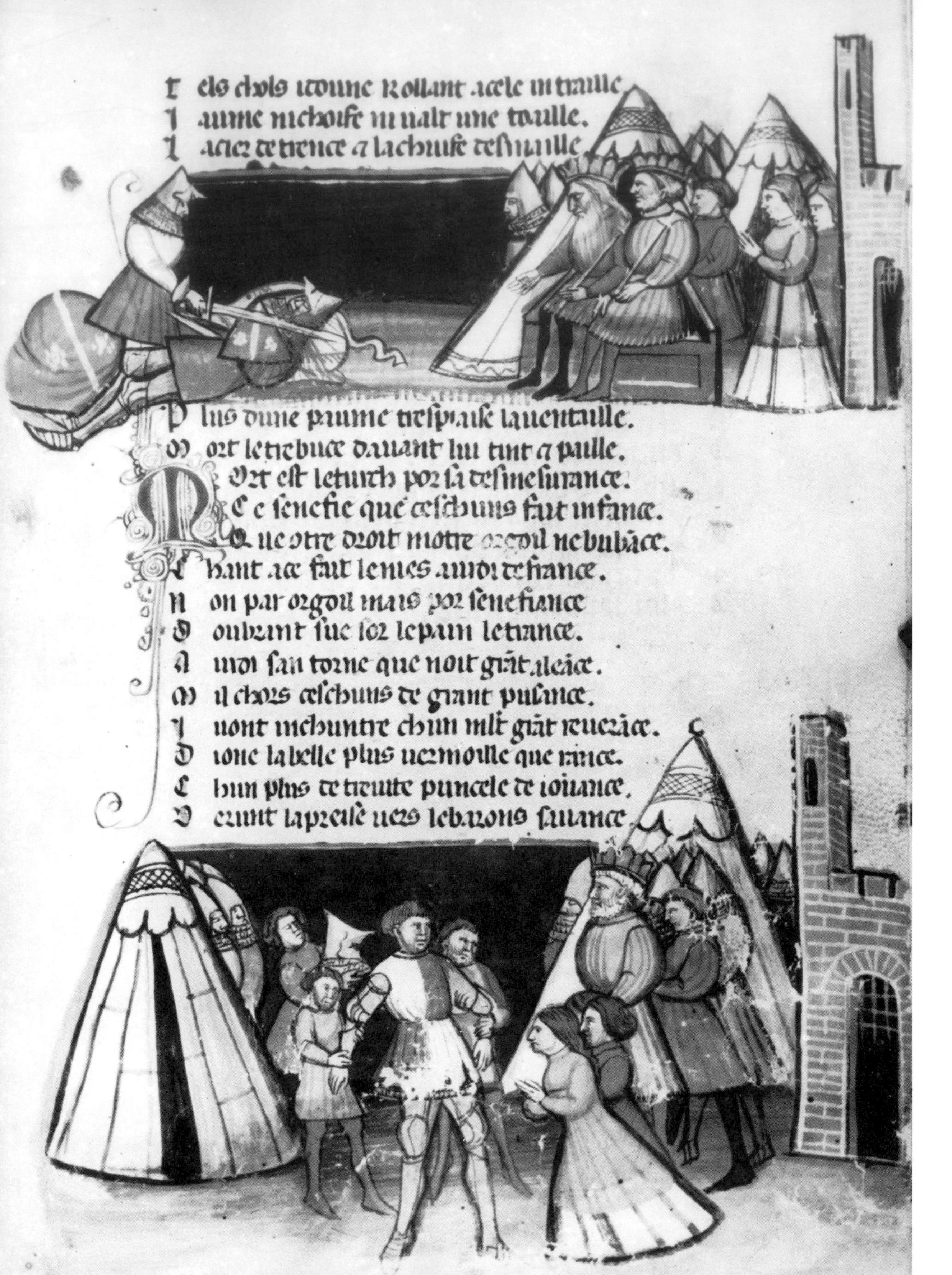
Tels cholps idonne Rollant a cele intraille
I aume ne choiffe ni valt une toaille.
I acier de tiente a la chausse desmaille
Plus d'une paume tresplaie la ventaille.
Mort le trebuche davant lui tant a paille.
Mort est le turch por sa desmesurance.
Ce senefie que ceschuns faut in fance.
Que otre droit motre orgoil ne bubance.
Chant ace faut le nies au roi de france.
Non par orgoil mais por senefiance
Doubrant sue loz le pain le triance.
Au roi s'an torne que noit grant aleiance.
Mil chors ceschuns de grant pusance.
Iuont incheuntre chiun mlt grant reuerance.
Dione la belle plus uermoille que rince.
Chun plus de trente puncele de iouance.
Deuant la preisse uers le barons sauance.

108–9 Assuming the name of Lionés fils de la Tré, Roland comes to the court of the Sultan of Persia and saves his daughter from marriage to an unwanted suitor. After further adventures, he returns to Charlemagne's court where he is affectionately welcomed by Oliver.

110–111 The *Pseudo-Turpin Chronicle* contains many details not in the Oxford version of the *Chanson de Roland.* At Roncevaux, Roland encounters a Saracen whom he ties to a tree and forces to point out Marsile. The heathen's military superiority is indicated by two cannon. To explain how the sound of Roland's horn reached Charlemagne over so vast a distance, he is shown blowing it high up in a tree.
After the battle, as he lies dying, he is found by his half-brother Baldwin who brings him water.

112–113 While the battle of Roncevaux is being fought, Turpin is saying Mass for Charlemagne and has a vision of the disaster. Thierry then arrives with news of the defeat and Roland's body is found (see Plate 21). A legend not mentioned in the *Pseudo-Turpin* concerns the miracle by which the bodies of the Christians were distinguished from those of the Saracens. Thorns grew from the heathen corpses, and lilies sprang from the Christians. In the bottom register, another miracle is taking place: Charles and Aude mourn over the long grave of the martyrs and a blind man and a cripple have been healed by touching the coffin.

Charlemaine 113

Ci commence le v.e livre charlemaine premierement de la traÿson que guenelon pourchaça.

Puis que charlemaine le tres
puissant & tresrenomme empereur
eut conquise toute la terre
de spaigne & galice & soubz
mise a la foy crestienne en lo
neur de dieu & de monseigneur saint iacques
Il retourna en france & fist ses ostz herbergier
delez la bonne cite de pampelune En cellui

◀ XXIV
Jean Fouquet's beautiful miniature shows Roland lying dead as Baldwin mourns him.

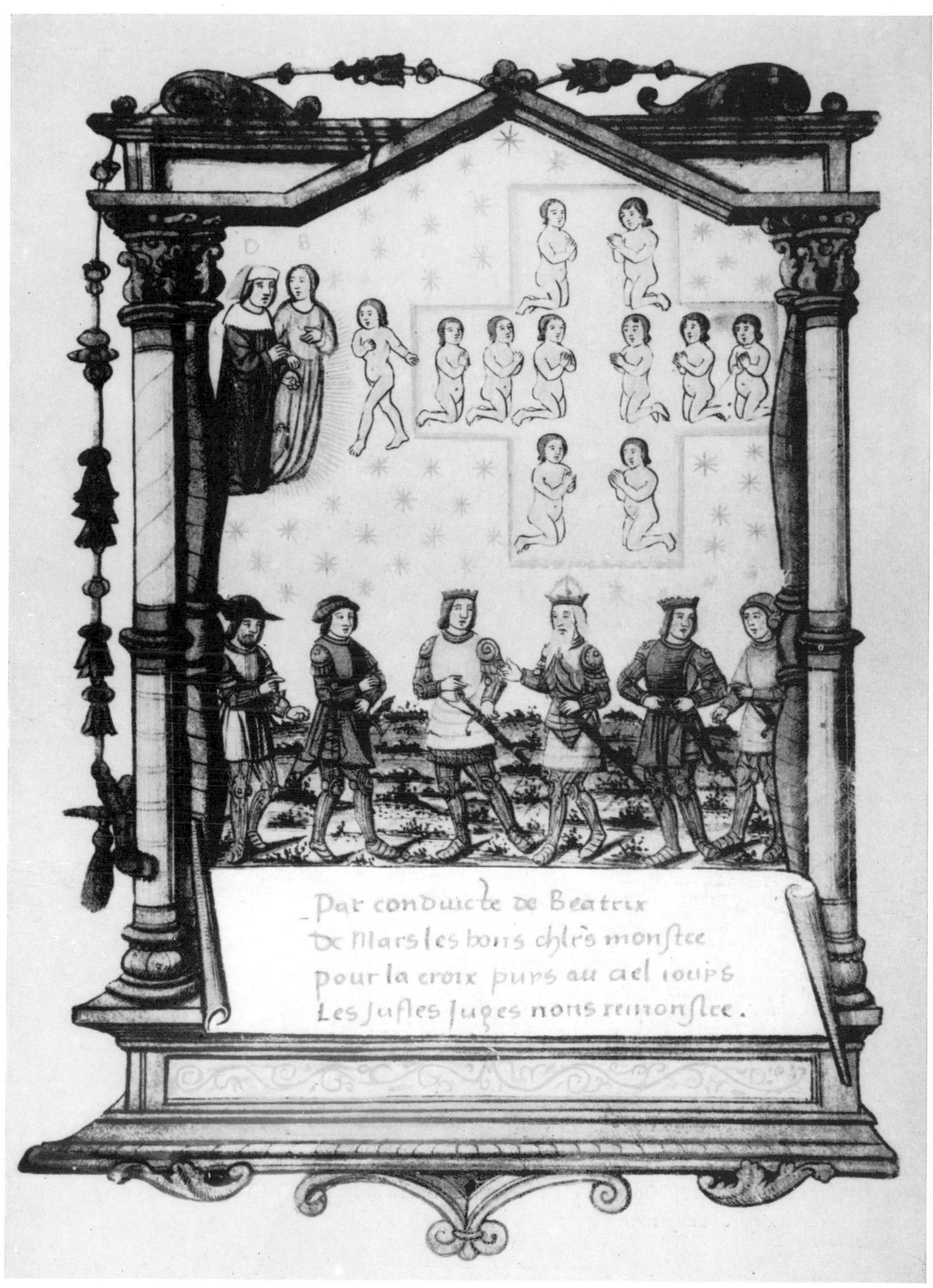

Par conduicte de Beatrix
De Mars les bons chlrs monstre
pour la croix purs au ciel loups
Les justes juges nons remonstre.

114 Roland and Charlemagne are shown in an illustration of the *Divine Comedy* in the fifth Heaven of Paradise.

115 Roland and Oliver armed as soldier saints stand guard on the pilgrim route to Compostela. Behind are four foundations of Charlemagne's dedicated to St. James.

Further Reading

An extensive detailed bibliography will be found in the Notes to Rita Lejeune and Jacques Stiennon, *La Légende de Roland dans l'art du moyen âge* (Brussels, 2 vols., 1966; English translation by Christine Trollope, London, Phaidon Press, 1971).

The standard edition of the Oxford *Chanson de Roland*, with modern French translation, is by Joseph Bédier (Paris, 1921). English verse translation by D.D.R. Owen, *The Song of Roland* (London, Unwin Books, 1972). Major studies include Pierre Le Gentil, *La Chanson de Roland* (Paris, 2nd edn. 1967; English translation by Frances F. Beer, Oxford, 1969), and Ramón Menéndez Pidal, *La Chanson de Roland et la tradition épique des Francs*, 2nd edn. translated from the Spanish by I.-M. Cluzel (Paris, 1960).

For the *Pseudo-Turpin Chronicle* see: C. Meredith-Jones, *Historia Karoli Magni et Rotholandi ou Chronique du Pseudo-Turpin* (Paris, 1936); H.M. Smyser, *The Pseudo-Turpin . . . with an Annotated Synopsis* (Cambridge, Mass., 1937).

General surveys of the legends include: Gaston Paris, *Histoire poétique de Charlemagne* (Paris, 1865); Jessie Crosland, *The Old French Epic* (Oxford, 1951).

Among the many works on the historical background are: Margaret Deanesly, *A History of Early Medieval Europe 476-911* (London, 2nd edn. 1960); J.M. Wallace-Hadrill, *The Long-Haired Kings and other Studies* (London, 1962); Peter Lasko, *The Kingdom of the Franks: North-West Europe before Charlemagne* (London, 1971); Donald Bullough, *The Age of Charlemagne* (London, 1965); *Einhard and Notker the Stammerer: Two Lives of Charlemagne*, translated by Lewis Thorpe (London, Penguin Classics, 1969); W. Montgomery Watt, *A History of Islamic Spain* (Edinburgh, 1965).

List of Plates

BLACK AND WHITE PLATES

20 Roland. Stone sculpture, *c.* 1420. Dubrovnik, market-place.

21 The story of Roncevaux. Miniature by Simon Marmion, *c.* 1460. *Les Grandes Chroniques de France.* Leningrad, Public Library, Ms fr.F.v.IV.1, fol. 154 r.

22 Roland slays Marsile. Tapestry woven in Tournai (detail), 1455–70. London, Victoria and Albert Museum.

23 Ganelon as Charles's emissary. Miniature, late 14th century. *Les Grandes Chroniques de France.* Paris, Bibl. Nat., Ms f.fr. 20350, fol. 109 v.

24 Communion of Roland. Stone sculpture, 1250–1290. Rheims, cathedral, interior wall of west end.

25 Conversion of the heathen. Miniature, 14th century. *Karl der Grosse* of Der Stricker. Wolfenbüttel, Herzog-August Bibliothek, Ms 1.5.2. August 2°, fol. 179 r.

26 Charles, Roland and Oliver. Pen-drawing, 1180–90. *Ruolantes Liet* of Conrad the Priest. Heidelberg, Universitätsbibliothek, Ms Pal. Germ. 112, fol. 5 v.

27 Marsile's first embassy to Charlemagne. Miniatures, *c.* 1350. *L'Entrée d'Espagne.* Venice, Bibl. Marciana, cod. fr. XXI, fol. 8 r.

28–29 Marsile's emissaries; council of the Franks. Pen and wash, *c.* 1450. *Karl der Grosse* of Der Stricker. Bonn, Universitätsbibliothek, Ms S.500, fol. 17 r., 30 r.

30 Charlemagne and Ganelon. Historiated initial, late 13th century. *Speculum Historiale* of Vincent of Beauvais. Madrid, Escorial, Ms O1.4., fol. 1 v.

31 West front of Aix-la-Chapelle Cathedral.

32 Ganelon drops Charlemagne's glove. Pen-drawing, 1180–90. *Ruolantes Liet* of Conrad the Priest. Heidelberg, Universitätsbibliothek, Ms Pal. Germ. 112, fol. 19 r.

33 Ganelon sets out for Saragossa. Pen and wash, *c.* 1450. *Karl der Grosse* of Der Stricker. Bonn, Universitätsbibliothek, Ms S.500, fol. 37 v.

34 Marsile and Ganelon ride outside Saragossa. Grisaille by Le Tavernier, *c.* 1460. *Chroniques et Conquestes de Charlemaine* of David Aubert. Brussels, Bibl. Royale, Ms 9067, fol. 252 v.

35 Marsile swears an oath by his idol. Pen-drawing, 1180–90. *Ruolantes Liet* of Conrad the Priest. Heidelberg, Universitätsbibliothek, Ms Pal. Germ. 112, fol. 32 v.

36 Ganelon swears an oath on his sword. Pen and wash, *c.* 1450. *Karl der Grosse* of Der Stricker. Bonn, Universitätsbibliothek, Ms S.500, fol. 41 v.

37 Marsile inspects the gifts for Charlemagne. Pen and wash, *c.* 1450. *Karl der Grosse* of Der Stricker. Bonn, Universitätsbibliothek, Ms S.500, fol. 48 v.

38 The gifts from Saragossa. Miniature, early 15th century. *Les Grandes Chroniques de France.* Brussels, Bibl. Royale, Ms 3, fol. 109 v., col. 1.

39 The gifts presented to Charles. Miniature, *c.* 1350. *Les Grandes Chroniques de France.* London, British Museum, Ms Royal 16 G VI, fol. 175 v.

40 Ganelon presents the gifts to Charles. Grisaille by Le Tavernier, *c.* 1460. *Chroniques et Conquestes de Charlemaine* of David Aubert. Brussels, Bibl. Royale, Ms 9067, fol. 238 v.

41 Saracen ambush. Miniature, *c.* 1345. *Karl der Grosse* of Der Stricker. Berlin, Deutsche Staatsbibliothek, Ms Germ. Fol. 623, fol. 21 v. (Ms now in Tübingen, Universitätsbibliothek.)

42 Charlemagne's prophetic dreams. Miniature, *c.* 1290. *Karl der Grosse* of Der Stricker. St. Gall, Stadtbibliothek, Ms 302, fol. 25 r.

43 Roland is appointed captain of the rearguard. Pen and wash, *c.* 1450. *Karl der Grosse* of Der Stricker. Bonn, Universitätsbibliothek, Ms S.500, fol. 54 r.

84 Charlemagne embraces Roland before knighting him. Wash drawing, *c.* 1200–50. *Chanson d'Aspremont.* London, British Museum, Ms Lansdowne 782, fol. 22 v.

85 Charles at the knighting ceremony for Roland. Wash drawing, 1200–50. *Chanson d'Aspremont.* London, British Museum, Ms Lansdowne 782, fol. 23 v.

86 Roland's first exploits as a knight. Grisaille by Le Tavernier, *c.* 1460. *Chroniques et Conquestes de Charlemaine* of David Aubert. Brussels, Bibl. Royale, Ms 9066, fol. 326 v.

87 Roland on his horse. Stone sculpture, *c.* 1200. Borgo San Donnino (Fidenza), Cathedral façade.

88 Roland's first encounter with Aude and Oliver at the siege of Vienne. Grisaille by Le Tavernier, *c.* 1460. *Chroniques et Conquestes de Charlemaine* of David Aubert. Brussels, Bibl. Royale, Ms. 9066, fol. 367 v.

89 Fighting during the siege of Vienne. Grisaille by Le Tavernier, *c.* 1460. *Chroniques et Conquestes de Charlemaine* of David Aubert. Brussels, Bibl. Royale, Ms 9066, fol. 386 r.

90 Betrothal of Roland and Aude. Grisaille by Le Tavernier, *c.* 1460. *Chroniques et Conquestes de Charlemaine* of David Aubert. Brussels, Bibl. Royale, Ms 9067, fol. 193 r.

91 Aude comes to Charlemagne for news of Roland. Grisaille by Le Tavernier, *c.* 1460. *Chroniques et Conquestes de Charlemaine* of David Aubert. Brussels, Bibl. Royale, Ms 9068, fol. 59 v.

92 Maugis making off with the peers' swords. Miniature by Loyset Liédet, *c.* 1460. *Renaut de Montauban.* Paris, Bibl. Nat., Ms Rés. 5072, fol. 271 r.

93 Roland and the peers captured by the Saracen King Balan. Grisaille by Le Tavernier, *c.* 1460. *Chroniques et Conquestes de Charlemaine* of David Aubert. Brussels, Bibl. Royale, Ms 9067, fol. 44 v.

94 Roland as Charlemagne's champion. Miniature by Loyset Liédet, 1462. *Chronique* of Baudouin d'Avesnes. Paris, Bibl. de l'Arsenal, Ms 5089, fol. 168 v.

95 Roland and Charlemagne before the True Cross at Jerusalem. Miniature, early 14th century. *Pseudo-Turpin Chronicle.* Florence, Bibl. Laurenziana, Ms Ashburnham 52, fol. 121 v.

96 The miraculous fall of Pamplona. Metalwork, 1200–15. Reliquary Châsse of St. Charlemagne. Aix-la-Chapelle, Cathedral treasury.

97 The city of Luiserne is engulfed. Miniature, *c.* 1325–50. *Les Grandes Chroniques de France.* London, British Museum, Ms Royal 16 G VI, fol. 166 r.

98 Charlemagne besieging Agen. Miniature, *c.* 1325–50. *Les Grandes Chroniques de France.* London, British Museum, Ms Royal 16 G VI, fol. 168 r.

99 Coronation of Charlemagne and final battle with Agolant. Miniature by Simon Marmion, *c.* 1455. *La Fleur des Histoires* of Jean Mansel. Brussels, Bibl. Royale, Ms 9232, vol. II, fol. 337 v.

100 Roland carried off by Ferragut. Miniature, *c.* 1350. *L'Entrée d'Espagne.* Venice, Bibl. Marciana, cod. fr. XXI, fol. 34 r.

101 Roland fighting Ferragut. Miniature, *c.* 1325–50. *Les Grandes Chroniques de France.* London, British Museum, Ms Royal 16 G VI, fol. 172 v.

102 Roland fighting Ferragut. Miniature, *c.* 1350. *L'Entrée d'Espagne.* Venice, Bibl. Marciana, cod. fr. XXI, fol. 44 r.

103 Roland fighting Ferragut on foot. Miniature, *c.* 1350. *L'Entrée d'Espagne.* Venice, Bibl. Marciana, cod. fr. XXI, fol. 64 v.

104 Roland placing a stone as a pillow below Ferragut's head. Miniature, *c.* 1350. *L'Entrée d'Espagne.* Venice, Bibl. Marciana, cod. fr. XXI, fol. 68 r.

105 Roland slays Ferragut. Grisaille by Le Tavernier, *c.* 1460. *Chroniques et Conquestes de Charlemaine* of David Aubert. Brussels, Bibl. Royale, Ms 9067, fol. 227 v.

106 Incident at the siege of Pamplona. Miniature, *c.* 1350. *L'Entrée d'Espagne.* Venice, Bibl. Marciana, cod. fr. XXI, fol. 176 r.

107 Roland struck by Charlemagne. Miniature, *c.* 1350. *L'Entrée d'Espagne.* Venice, Bibl. Marciana, cod. fr. XXI, fol. 216 r.

108 Roland at the court of the Sultan of Persia. Miniature, *c.* 1350. *L'Entrée d'Espagne.* Venice, Bibl. Marciana, cod. fr. XXI, fol. 254 r.

109 Roland returns to Charlemagne and Oliver. Miniature, *c.* 1350. *L'Entrée d'Espagne.* Venice, Bibl. Marciana, cod. fr. XXI, fol. 296 v.

110 Roland ties a Saracen to a tree. Miniature, 1515–25. *Recueil sommaire des cronicques françoyses* of Guillaume Cretin. Paris, Bibl. Nat., Ms f. fr. 1820, fol. 124 r.

111 Baldwin bringing Roland water. Miniature, early 14th century. *Pseudo-Turpin Chronicle.* Florence, Bibl. Laurenziana, Ms Ashburnham 52, fol. 132 v.

112 Vision of Turpin. Miniature, *c.* 1325–50. *Les Grandes Chroniques de France.* London, British Museum, Ms Royal 16 G VI, fol. 180 v.

113 Miracles concerning the dead of Roncevaux. Miniature, *c.* 1290. *Karl der Grosse* of Der Stricker. St. Gall, Stadtbibliothek, Ms 302, fol. 71 r.

114 Roland and Charlemagne in the fifth Heaven. Miniature, 15th century. *Divine Comedy,* French translation by François Bergagne. Paris, Bibl. Nat., nouv. acq. fr. 4119, fol. 101 v.

115 Roland and Oliver as guardians of the pilgrim routes. Pen and wash, late 15th century. *Pseudo-Turpin Chronicle.* Paris, Bibl. Nat., Ms f. fr. 4991, fol. 8 v.

COLOUR PLATES

I Charlemagne between Roland and Oliver. Stained glass, *c.* 1200 from Strasbourg Cathedral. Strasbourg, Musée de l'Œuvre de Notre Dame.

II Charlemagne's army set out for Spain; the returning warriors at Aix. Miniature, late 12th century. *Codex Calixtinus.* Compostela, Cathedral archive, fol. 162 v.

III Battle of Roncevaux. Miniature, 1493. *Les Grandes Chroniques de France.* Paris, Antoine Vérard, 1493. Paris, Bibl. Nat., Ms Rés. vélin 725.

IV Miracle of the flowering lances. Metalwork, 1200–15. Reliquary Châsse of St. Charlemagne. Aix-la-Chapelle, Cathedral treasury.

V Roland sounds his horn. Pen and wash by Diebolt Lauber, *c.* 1450. *Karl der Grosse* of Der Stricker. Bonn, Universitätsbibliothek, Ms S.500, fol. 136 r.

VI Charlemagne and the hostages from Saragossa; Roland attacks Marsile. Miniatures, 1375–9. *Les Grandes Chroniques de France.* Paris, Bibl. Nat., Ms f. fr. 2813, fol. 121 r.

Index

Numbers in *italics* refer to black and white Plates, roman numerals refer to colour Plates.